Prisons: A Study in Vulnerability

GS Misc 557

Prisons: A Study in Vulnerability

A collection of essays
from the
Board for Social Responsibility

CHURCH HOUSE
PUBLISHING

Church House Publishing
Church House
Great Smith Street
London
SW1P 3NZ

ISBN 0 7151 6584 4

Published in 1999 for the Board for Social Responsibility of the Church of England by Church House Publishing.

You have to pray daily, light a candle — get down on your knees — as far as prisons are concerned.

Jack Straw, Home Secretary, March 1999

To open eyes that are blind, to bring captives out of prison, out of the dungeons where they lie in darkness.

Isaiah 42.7 (NEB)

Contents

III. The Christian Response

List of Photographs

Contributors

Mr Paul Cavadino is Director of Policy of the National Association for the Care and Resettlement of Offenders (NACRO) and Chair of the Penal Affairs Consortium.

Dr Ian Cummings is Forensic Psychiatrist at HM Prison Belmarsh.

The Ven David Fleming is Chaplain General to Prisons.

Ms Lucy Gampell is Director of the Federation of Prisoners' Families Support Groups.

Ms Janet Harber is Chair of the Federation of Prisoners' Families Support Groups.

The Rt Revd Robert Hardy is Bishop to Prisons.

Mr Martin Narey is Director General of the Prison Service.

Mr Tim Newell is Governor of HM Prison Grendon.

Ms Fran Russell is Assistant Director of the Howard League for Penal Reform.

The Revd Dr Peter Sedgwick is Assistant Secretary, Board for Social Responsibility.

Ms Clare Sparks is Policy Officer with the Prison Reform Trust.

Mr John Wrigglesworth is an inmate in HM Prison Grendon.

Foreword

This is not a usual report to General Synod from a working party set up by a board or council. The Board for Social Responsibility has excellent relationships with staff in the Prison Service and with agencies outside the Service, who work for change and who support the vulnerable. The Home Affairs Committee, chaired by the Bishop of Lincoln, who is also Bishop to Prisons, decided to invite some of these people to contribute to a collection of essays on the theme of 'vulnerability' inside prisons today. The purpose is to inform members of General Synod, and the general public, about what it means to be a vulnerable person caught up in the Prison System, and so help bring about greater compassion and understanding for an often forgotten group of people. We are grateful to all those who contributed essays in the midst of busy lives. This collection is authorized by the Board for Social Responsibility as a contribution to debate, but the Board does not endorse the views expressed by individual contributors.

✠ Richard Harries
Bishop of Oxford
Chair, Board for Social Responsibility

Acknowledgements

Our thanks are due to the *Church Times*, who authorized us to use the report on Christopher Edwards by Sarah Meyrick; and to the Prison Reform Trust for allowing us to use their photographic material.

Introduction

Life in prison is a closed world to the majority of people, yet it has a profound effect on those, who, for whatever reason, come into contact with it. It contains many of those problems which affect contemporary society, yet hides from view numerous situations which few are prepared to face.[1]

In these essays we have tried to give a series of snapshots of some of the aspects of prison today. It is easy to despair in the face of much that is set out here, but that is not an option for us. The Prison Service has done much in recent years to develop constructive regimes for those detained, and there is a real willingness on the part of both professionals and volunteers to build on good practice, and to see continuing improvements made to our Prison System. What is needed now is more informed opinion, the will to explore initiatives and alternatives to prison, and the continuing support of prayer and concern for all those working with offenders and their families.

✠ Robert Hardy
Bishop of Lincoln
Bishop to Prisons

I

The State of Prisons Today

1

Punishing the Vulnerable

A Statistical Overview of Recent Trends in Sentencing and Imprisonment

Paul Cavadino

The evidence of vulnerable characteristics among people in prison is extensive and widely documented. For example:

- The Home Office's National Prison Survey 1991 found that 26 per cent of prisoners, and 38 per cent of those under 21, had spent time in local authority care; 33 per cent had been unemployed and 13 per cent homeless before imprisonment; and 30 per cent said that they had mostly truanted from school after the age of 11.

- A study by the Office of National Statistics of prisoners' psychiatric problems, published in 1998, found that the proportion of prisoners with 'significant neurotic psychopathology' ranged from 39 per cent of sentenced male prisoners to 75 per cent of female remand prisoners.

- A series of studies by Professor John Gunn and his colleagues at the Institute of Psychiatry, published between 1990 and 1992, found that 11 per cent of male and 23 per cent of female prisoners were drug dependent, defining 'dependence' as daily use before imprisonment, withdrawal symptoms on abstinence and an acceptance by the prisoner that he or she was dependent.

- Research cited in the Prison Service Corporate Plan for 1999–2000 to 2000–2002 has shown that the literacy and numeracy skills of 60 per cent of prisoners are at Basic Skill Level 1 or below, depriving them of the opportunity to apply for many jobs on release.

- A survey of women prisoners by HM Chief Inspector of Prisons, published in 1997, found that 70 per cent had been unemployed before entering prison; 36 per cent had serious educational problems; 20 per cent had been in care; nearly half had been physically or sexually abused; 40 per cent reported heavy use of or addiction to drugs; and over 40 per cent had deliberately harmed themselves or attempted suicide.

- A study of young prisoners by HM Chief Inspector of Prisons published in 1997 found that over half had been excluded from school; two-thirds had been unemployed before imprisonment; almost two-thirds had misused drugs; 17 per cent had suffered abuse; and over half of those aged under 18 had a history of care or social services contact.

Against this background, the growing harshness reflected in recent sentencing trends represents a substantial increase in the punishment of many vulnerable offenders.

Recent trends

At end of July 1998, the prison population of England and Wales stood at a record 66,516. It had risen by 64 per cent since the end of 1992 when it was 40,606. There had been an even sharper percentage rise in the number of women prisoners, which was 3,189 – an increase of 136 per cent since the end of 1992 when it was 1,353. The number of young prisoners had risen by 72 per cent, from 6,783 to 11,636.

Since then, there has been a fall in the prison population, principally because of the introduction on 28 January 1999 of a new scheme for the early release of selected prisoners under a home detention curfew monitored by electronic tagging. In mid-April 1999 there were 2,074 prisoners under home detention curfews. The population of prisons was 63,945, comprising 60,776 males and 3,169 females. Even after this fall, the prison population was still 57 per cent higher, and in the case of women 132 per cent higher, than at the end of 1992.

The rising prison population is not due to an increase in the number of offenders appearing before the courts, but is due to harsher sentencing. At all courts, the proportion of adult offenders sentenced for indictable offences who were sentenced to immediate custody rose from 16 per cent in 1992 to 25 per cent in 1997. At the Crown Court the proportion rose from 45 per cent to 61 per cent, while at magistrates' courts it increased from 5 to 11 per cent. The average length of sentence has also increased. The average sentence length at the Crown Court rose from 21.1 months in 1992 to 24.2 months in 1997 for adult males and from 17.7 months to 19.5 months for adult females. Increases have occurred for most categories of offence.

In a speech to the National Probation Convention on 12 November 1997, the Lord Chief Justice, Lord Bingham of Cornhill, said:

> It is a fact very well known to us all that there has in recent years been an exponential increase in the prison population . . . The reason for this exponential increase is, I have no doubt, the vocal expression of opinion by influential public figures that custody is an effective penalty. In contrast with a decade ago, when the efficacy of community penalties was widely canvassed, the emphasis has been on custody as *the* effective disposal in cases of other than minor crime.

The emphasis to which Lord Bingham was referring was clearly that of leading politicians, most notably the 'prison works' rhetoric of Michael Howard during his tenure as Home Secretary from 1993 to 1997.

The current prison population of around 64,000 means that this country has 122 prisoners for every 100,000 people in the general population, compared with 110 in Spain, 90 in France and Germany, 85 in Italy and Holland, 80 in Belgium, 65 in Denmark, 60 in Sweden, 55 in Norway and 50 in Greece. In the whole of Western Europe, only Portugal jails a higher proportion of its population than ourselves. Not only are we readier to jail offenders than most of our West European neighbours; we also have a higher prison population than many developing countries. For example, the median imprisonment rate for Western and Central Africa is 60; for South America 110; and for South Central Asia (which mainly comprises the Indian subcontinent) 45.

Most of the people we send to prison are non-violent offenders: around 70 per cent of those imprisoned during 1997 had committed offences which did not involve violence, sex, robbery or drug trafficking. Of 80,832 offenders sentenced to imprisonment during that year:

11,713 (14 per cent) had committed violent offences

2,498 (3 per cent) had committed sexual offences

3,784 (5 per cent) had committed robbery

7,074 (9 per cent) had committed drugs offences

11,700 (14 per cent) had committed burglary

16,985 (21 per cent) had committed theft and handling offences

2,839 (4 per cent) had committed fraud or forgery

12,287 (15 per cent) had committed motoring offences

10,043 (12 per cent) had committed other offences

in 1,119 cases (1 per cent) the offence was not recorded in prison statistics.

Not only does the increasing use of prison punish the vulnerable more severely, but it also increases their vulnerability. In a large-scale resettlement survey carried out by the National Association for the Care and Resettlement of Offenders (NACRO) in 1992, 55 per cent of prisoners taking part had been unemployed before imprisonment but a further 34 per cent said that they had lost their jobs because of the sentences. Whereas 13 per cent of prisoners were homeless before imprisonment, a further 34 per cent had lost their homes through being in prison. A third of prisoners said that they had lost contact with family and friends because of being in prison, and the proportion of prisoners reporting loss of such community ties increased in direct proportion to the longer time they had spent in prison. Yet prisoners who are released jobless, homeless and without family support are much more likely to reoffend.

Imprisonment disproportionately affects black and Asian offenders, who are more likely to be jailed than comparable white offenders. Minority ethnic groups make up 5.5 per cent of the general population, yet in the prison population of England and Wales the proportion is 18 per cent of all prisoners and 25 per cent of female prisoners. However, in the London area and in some other large cities, the figure can be much higher in local prisons and in Young Offenders Institutions. On release, black and Asian offenders often face problems of discrimination additional to those faced by others with the stigma of a criminal record.

The impact on prisons

The growing pressure of numbers is felt most sharply in the country's town and city centre local prisons. On 31 January 1999 male local prisons, which had 19,691 places, were holding a total of 23,614 prisoners: on average they were 20 per cent overcrowded. However, some prisons are much more overcrowded than the average. On the same date, 12 prisons were over 30 per cent overcrowded, eight of which were over 40 per cent overcrowded. Six had overcrowding of over 50 per cent, four of over 60 per cent, two of over 70 per cent and one of 90 per cent. The number of prisoners held two to a cell designed for one person rose from 8,426 in 1994–5 to 11,584 in 1997–8.

In the first half of the 1990s, despite the pressure of increasing numbers, the Prison Service improved its performance by increasing the number of hours prisoners spent out of their cells and in constructive activity, ending slopping out and eliminating the 'trebling' of prisoners in cells. Subsequent events, however, placed these achievements in jeopardy as a result of a continuing sharp rise in the prison population together with the imposition on the Prison Service of substantial budget cuts.

The Prison Service Corporate Plan for 1999–2000 to 2001–2 (March 1999) stated that significant improvements had been made in creating a decent environment in prisons in recent years, but added:

> . . . the unprecedented increase in the prison population over the last few years has resulted in serious overcrowding, particularly in local prisons, and the number of prisoners doubled – two prisoners in a cell designed for one – remains high. This is a particular problem where in-cell sanitation is not adequately separated from the living area. More importantly overcrowding presents risks to the stability of any establishment because of the pressures it puts on regimes, staff and prison resources.

As a result of efficiency savings and budget cuts, between 1992 and 1993 the cost per uncrowded prisoner place was cut by 9.6 per cent and is estimated to have fallen by 10.1 per cent by the end of 1997–8. Cost per prisoner fell by 25.3 per cent over the five years to 1998. Detailed decisions on how cuts are to be made in each prison were left to individual prison governors. The effects of the cuts in Prison Service budgets included:

- Reductions in staffing. As a result of early exit schemes in 1996–7, the number of prison officers in post fell from 24,398 in 1996 to 23,058 in 1997 at a time of growing prisoner numbers.

- A reduction in prison education. 84 per cent of prisons cut their number of education hours in 1996–7, 56 per cent did so in 1997–8 and 71 per cent did so in 1998–9. The average number of education hours per prisoner fell from 4.9 hours in 1995–6 to 3.8 hours in the first quarter of 1998–9. The Chief Inspector of Prisons commented in his Annual Report for 1996–7:

If any aspect of the inspection process depresses my inspectors it is the number of times that they have to report the effect of cuts in work and education in prisons, meaning that prisoners are left locked in their cells because there is nothing for them to do . . . Cuts in work and education have not resulted from a deliberate policy imposed by Ministers or Prison Service Headquarters, who I know regret them as much as anyone. But they are the inevitable result of imposing cuts on Governors of prisons, which rapidly need to be brought into effect and having no other options available.

- Prisoners spending increased time locked in their cells. The percentage of prisoners held in prisons which unlocked inmates for 12 or more hours per weekday fell from 40 per cent in 1994–5 to 37.5 per cent in 1995–6. In 1996–7 the Prison Service changed its key performance indicator for time unlocked, so that it measured the percentage of prisoners held in prisons which unlocked those on standard and enchanced regimes for 10 or more hours per weekday (not 12 hours as previously). The percentage fell from 65 per cent in 1996–7 to 62 per cent in 1997–8 and the Prison Service's target for 1998–9 was 60 per cent. A reduction in the level of purposeful activity in prisons fell from an average of 26.2 hours per prisoner per week in 1994–5 to 23.3 hours in 1997–8. The Prison Service's target in both 1998–9 and 1999–2000 was to increase this to 24 hours a week.

The number of prisoners completing programmes accredited as being effective in reducing reoffending increased from 1,371 in 1996–7 to a planned 3,000 in 1998–9 (including 680 completions of sex offender treatment programmes). However, such programmes as yet cover only a small proportion of the prison population.

A further result of the sharp increase in the prison population has been 'the constant movement of prisoners around the system to ensure the optimal use of the prison estate, often far from their homes and disrupting their sentence and preparation for release plans' (HM Prison Service, *Prison Service Review*, October 1997).

The overall trend was assessed as follows by Sir David Ramsbotham, HM Chief Inspector of Prisons, in his Annual Report for 1996–7. He pointed out that, while money had been made available to increase levels of security:

> . . . it has been cut, and continues to be cut, despite the provision of some extra financial resources, from activities designed to help prisoners to lead law-abiding and useful lives in custody and after release. Probation services have been cut, both in the number of seconded staff working in prisons, and staff to supervise prisoners on release. Education has been cut in virtually every prison, for financial reasons. There is no laid down minimum of education provision, except for those of under school leaving age, and even their statutory needs are not being met in all cases. There is not enough work in too many prisons, because instructor posts have been cut and workshops closed. Psychologists, who design and help to run offending behaviour treatment programmes, have been cut. Prison staff, trained in resettlement work, are all too often required on other duties since numbers have been cut, and so too many prisoners leave prison without proper preparation for release . . . In sum, while money and attention have been directed at the security part of the mission, the reverse has been true of the rehabilitation.

Government plans

A series of actions have been taken or are currently planned by the Government and the Prison Service to address these problems. On 13 February 1998 the Home Secretary announced an additional £112 million funding for the Prison Service for 1998–9 to help meet population pressures. On 21 July 1998, following the Government's Comprehensive

Spending Review, he announced a further £660 million over the three years from 1999–2000 to 2001–2 for additional prison capacity, to clear the backlog of urgent repair and maintenance, and for a 'significant increase in purposeful activity'. The latter, which will amount to over £200 million over three years, will be directed principally to three areas: programmes to reduce substance misuse, accredited offending behaviour programmes and improving basic skills. As a result of the Comprehensive Spending Review settlement, there will be a modest increase in real term costs per uncrowded prison place of 0.9 per cent over the three years.

A Director of Regimes was appointed from January 1998, with Assistant Directors responsible for regimes in adult training prisons, Young Offenders Institutions and women's prisons. The Prison Service has adopted targets of:

- reducing by 15 per cent the proportion of discharged prisoners who are at level 1 or below for literacy and numeracy skills by April 2002;

- increasing the number of accredited offending behaviour programmes run by the Prison Service from 3,000 to 6,000 a year by 2001–2, including an increase from 680 to 1,100 in those completing sex offender treatment programmes;

- establishing a separate estate with enhanced regimes for males over 18 and establishing young offender units for young female prisoners;

- increasing from 11 to 14 the number of establishments running Welfare to Work programmes over the next three years;

- improving the assessment, support and resettlement of drug misusing prisoners, improving the availability of quality drug treatment and providing opportunities for all prisoners to be located in voluntary testing units by April 2001.

Conclusion

Time will tell how effective the Government's current plans will prove to be in improving the treatment and rehabilitation of the many vulnerable people held within the Prison System. However, the Prison Service would undoubtedly have a far better prospect of doing so if the trend of the last six years towards markedly more punitive sentences could be arrested and reversed. Above all, we need to rediscover the enlightened message of Lord Woolf's report into the prison riots of 1990 (HMSO, 1991):

> Because it is under pressure, the Prison Service should not be required to hold more prisoners than is necessary. But, even if the overcrowding problem were to be solved it would still be important to ensure, so far as possible, that only those for whom there is no alternative are in prison. It is important to avoid subjecting anyone to the damaging effects of imprisonment unless this cannot be avoided . . . Any resources which need not be incurred in meeting the cost of housing prisoners who do not need to be imprisoned should be saved. The savings can then be used more constructively, for example in trying to counter offenders' criminal behaviour. It is therefore important, as is generally recognised, to reduce the prison population to an unavoidable minimum.

2

Improvements in Prison Regimes

Martin Narey

I believe prisons can be made to work. We can make them work as communities in their own right; that are safe, fair and responsible places to live and work. We can make them work as places that keep prisoners constructively engaged, challenging their lifestyles and looking ahead. And we can make them work as an element in a much bigger strategy for reducing crime.[1]

Rt Hon Jack Straw, July 1998

Introduction

The Government is committed to a policy of protecting the public and, to this end, to providing regimes in prisons which reduce the risk of reoffending.

The Prison Service has two key objectives, to:

- protect the public by holding those convicted by the courts in a safe, decent and healthy environment;

- reduce crime by providing constructive regimes which address offending behaviour, improve educational and work skills, and promote law-abiding behaviour in custody and after release.

The success in the last few years in meeting the first objective for public protection (with the consequent reduction in escapes) has allowed a renewed focus on regimes to meet the second objective: to help prisoners 'lead law-abiding lives in custody and after release'. But this should be seen as complementing and in no way replacing the ongoing attention to security.

Beyond that, regimes must be responsive to the needs of individual prisoners, particularly vulnerable groups. They must be designed to prepare and equip prisoners to lead responsible and offence-free lives when they return to the community.

This is not new; the Prison Service has had a long-standing commitment to provide constructive regimes for prisoners and there is a considerable array of good practice upon which to build.

This chapter describes some of the work under way to develop constructive regimes which can reduce the risk of reoffending. I cannot do justice here to all the work in progress in around 135 establishments in England and Wales. Instead, after a short description of the principles underpinning all the work we do, I have picked out developments relevant to two groups on which the Prison Service is currently focusing particular attention: women prisoners and young offenders aged under 18 years.

Constructive regimes

Constructive regimes must:

- focus continually on release and life in the community following release;

- be based on the evidence of what works in reducing reoffending;

- challenge the attitudes that lead to crime;

- offer opportunities to prisoners to make the choice not to reoffend and be effective in supporting that choice.

The basic components must include:

- rigorous individual assessment;

- meaningful work and training;

- education in basic skills;

- planning for employment;

- planning for accommodation outside prison;

- the opportunity to tackle substance abuse;

- targeted offending behaviour programmes for those that can benefit from them.

These are not only aspirational wishes for the Service. The Business Plan for the Criminal Justice System for 1999–2000, published in April 1999, includes as two specific objectives, targets for the provision of offending behaviour programmes and new challenging targets for improvements in prisoners' basic skills.

Assessment and sentence planning

The foundation for regime development has to be sound **assessments** of individual prisoners. The sentence management and planning system provides the framework for co-ordinating assessments of the individual. It gives a comprehensive assessment of a prisoner in relation to his/her offending, to risks they present to themselves or others, and in relation to needs, linked to reducing reoffending and effective resettlement. It, therefore, brings together a wide range of assessments – encompassing offending behaviour, drug abuse, education, employment, family issues and accommodation, as well as issues about a prisoner's ability to cope and vulnerability, for example to bullying.

The overall assessment then informs decisions about the management of the prisoner forming the basis of plans for the sentence and specific targets, for example about attending programmes and pursuing courses.

Assessment is a developing area and work is now under way, in collaboration with the Probation Service, to develop a joint 'risk/needs' assessment tool and a complementary framework to assess dangerousness. This work is drawing heavily on research and will be fully evaluated.

Work and education

Many prisoners have had poor educational experiences and their levels of literacy and numeracy are a real barrier to finding worthwhile employment. Nearly 60 per cent of prisoners are at Basic Skills Level 1 or below for literacy, and 75 per cent are at Level 1 or below for numeracy. The Basic Skills Agency estimates that this means that 60 per cent are ineligible for 96 in every 100 jobs. The importance of basic skills in helping to prevent reoffending is reflected in the target in our Business Plan for 1999–2000, to 'provide education in basic skills so that by April 2002, there will be a 15 per cent reduction in prisoners who are at Level 1 or below for literacy and numeracy skills'.

Education in prison is, therefore, focused on a core curriculum of basic educational skills, life and social skills and information technology. These are skills which the employment market demands. They are also fundamental in helping prisoners improve their self-esteem.

The Prison Service recognizes that education need not be delivered exclusively in the classroom in formal lessons. Many prisoners find it easier to understand and accept that they need help with basic skills when those needs are seen in the context of their work. As part of the new education strategy, all establishments must have plans identifying ways of supporting prisoners with basic skills needs in the workplace. Instructional Officers, who supervise prisoners in workshops, are being trained and accredited as basic skills support tutors. The Prison Service is working with the Basic Skills Agency to produce training material and training programmes for physical education (PE) officers to address basic skills needs through PE. These innovative approaches can be particularly effective with prisoners whose previous experiences make them less responsive to classroom-based learning.

Plate 1: Work is an integral part of the prison regime.
Mike Grieve, for the Prison Reform Trust.

Other recent developments include family literacy projects, in partnership with the Basic Skills Agency, and peer partnership projects, which will train prisoners to support others in areas such as basic skills and English for speakers of other languages. The family literacy projects, which are being developed at five Young Offenders Institutions and an establishment for women, help both prisoners and their children with reading, pre-reading and listening skills but also foster bonds between prisoners and their families. A new dyslexia awareness pack has been distributed to all prisons following a successful pilot of screening for dyslexia in dispersal (maximum security) prisons.

Work

Many prisoners have little experience of steady employment and the discipline of regular work habits. Work in prison aims to provide prisoners with the opportunity to acquire the attitudes and habits which are vital in retaining jobs. NVQ training in a wide variety of specific work skills is offered in prisons so that prisoners can gain qualifications which will enhance their employment prospects.

Major investment is being made in increasing the availability and range of work for prisoners. The aim is to make work in prisons more equivalent in tempo and hours with work in the outside world. A central sales and marketing team supports prisons' efforts to market themselves and so open up opportunities both to sell the goods they produce and attract new work from the private sector.

Welfare to Work

During the last two years, the Prison Service has also taken part in the Government's Welfare to Work initiative. Young ex-prisoners are a particularly hard-to-employ group and many of them face severe difficulties in finding work once they are discharged. Research findings show that 60 per cent of young prisoners are likely to have been unemployed previously and that 89 per cent of all prisoners become unemployed on release.

The Service has developed and piloted a Welfare to Work programme, which now runs in 15 prisons and Young Offenders Institutions. It provides intensive intervention in the last two or three months of sentence for 18- to 24-year-olds, seeking to improve their work skills and give them a better chance of success in the job market. It operates in partnership with the New Deal for 18- to 24-year-olds, which ex-offenders can join immediately on release.

The Prison Service programme provides job skill training, employment advice and support in preparation for work. Effective joint working between the Prison, Probation and Employment Services at the point of release is crucial, providing the transition to continued support after discharge.

By the end of the first year, 2,400 prisoners had joined the programme, and 1,500 had already completed it. It is heartening to report that participants were gaining new accredited job skills: they achieved an average of nearly six out of seven possible certificates, covering key skills in literacy and numeracy, practical qualifications in first aid and food hygiene and so on. There was also evidence that those taking part were twice as likely to join the New Deal Gateway on release, and thus continue to progress towards employment.

Welfare to Work has a further dimension: research indicates that ex-offenders with a stable job, or actively looking for work, are far less likely to reoffend. Home Office evaluation of the programme will provide information on both the success of inmates on release, and whether they have reoffended.

Offending behaviour programmes

Research literature, mostly from North America, provides firm evidence of the efficacy of programmes in prison which are designed to improve problem-solving and social interaction, and which include a cognitive component to address attitudes, values and beliefs which support offending behaviour. But this research also shows that to be successful, programmes must be properly carried out by trained staff in accordance with set aims and objectives. This means a tough system of accreditation of programmes to ensure that they are designed and delivered with rigorous adherence to the principles identified by the 'What Works' research.

The Prison Service now has two cognitive skills programmes running in over 70 establishments, one lasting for 35 sessions, and a shorter 20 session programme. We are evaluating the success of the programmes in improving cognitive skills and in the longer term on reducing reoffending. Early results are encouraging.

The Prison Service has also developed its own sex offender treatment programme based on the same cognitive-behavioural approaches. Run in 24 establishments, it is longer than the other programmes, and also provides individual and 'booster' sessions, designed to prevent relapse. Again, early results are very encouraging.

Indeed, Ministers are so convinced that these programmes can have a real impact on reoffending that the Prison Service has a target in the 1999–2000 Business Plan to:

> increase the numbers of completions by prisoners of offending behaviour programmes accredited as being effective in reducing reoffending from a target of 3,000 in 1998–9 to 3,600 in 1999–2000, of which 700 will be completions of sex offender treatment programmes.

I foresee even higher targets for future years.

Drug strategy

The Prison Service has an important role to play in the Government's strategy on drug issues, specifically the national strategy *Tackling Drugs to Build a Better Britain*. This means we must continue to work at reducing both the supply of, and demand for, illegal drugs, and at reducing the potential for damage to health associated with drug misuse. The programme of work for the next three years includes:

Treatment:	more intervention programmes by external agencies; accreditation of the programmes; more voluntary testing wings for prisoners wanting to be drug free;
Reduction:	supply improved methods for the prevention and detection of drug smuggling; inter-agency liaison with family support groups to provide advice and support for prisoners' friends and families;
Research:	into the needs of specific groups of offenders; into the effectiveness of the strategy.

Prisons and probation

Providing constructive regimes and preparing prisoners for responsible lives in the community requires close co-operation between the Prison and Probation Services. The two services are working closely together and have embarked upon a challenging and wide-ranging agenda to provide for greater effectiveness in their work together. This is focusing on practical ways in which the services achieve improvements in effective resettlement of prisoners. For example, as well as work to develop a joint risk and needs assessment tool, there will also be a common approach to programme accreditation and a project on developing information technology links between prisons and probation.

This is a general picture of provision for prisoners. But it cannot be the whole story because different groups of different prisoners have different needs and it is certainly not the case in regime design that 'one size fits all'. Other prisoner groups with particular needs include women prisoners, young offenders and offenders we describe as 'vulnerable' (some, but not all, sex offenders).

Race relations

The Prison Service is committed to treating prisoners fairly and a Prison Service Order sets out the mandatory and recommended standards which prisons must observe to ensure that no prisoner is discriminated against on the grounds of race, religion or ethnic origin. The Order covers all aspects of prison life from accommodation, work and education to diet, access to books and to appropriate goods on sale in prison shops. The Prison Service Race Relations statement is prominently displayed in key areas around every prison, and inmates, staff and visitors are expected to observe its principles.

Establishing a policy of equal treatment is just the first step; ensuring that the policy is put into effect requires leadership and commitment. Governors set the tone for race relations within an establishment and carry primary responsibility for ensuring that the policy is delivered. In a number of recent statements I have highlighted the importance of this leadership role.

At a day-to-day level, the Race Relations Liaison Officers (RRLOs) monitor the performance of their establishments against the standards laid down. The RRLO is also responsible for the difficult and sensitive task of ensuring that all racial incidents are properly recorded and investigated. They report on their work to the Race Relations Monitoring Team (RRMT), whose members are drawn from the key functional areas within the prison and will generally also include a representative from a local community organization. The RRMT draws up an action plan to address any areas of concern which are identified. Work is now going on to improve the effectiveness of these structures and procedures which are vital to the delivery of the Prison Service Race Relations policy. Encouragement of leadership from Governors, a greater degree of support for RRLOs and closer monitoring of the outcomes will all be used as levers to better performance.

Women prisoners

A priority group for the Prison Service in the last two years has been the rapidly growing number of women prisoners. In 1997 my predecessor acknowledged that their needs were not being met by the provision of specifically designed regimes. He, therefore, set up a group at Prison Headquarters with the objective of developing regimes specifically for women prisoners and female young offenders, and of ensuring that policy development in all aspects of prison life reflected the needs of women prisoners.

A high priority has been the establishment of improved regime pilots at Holloway and Styal prisons in 1998/9. £1.5 million has been made available to improve regimes for women and young female offenders in these two establishments. The provision of offending behaviour programmes is a core element of the pilots, as is education – with an emphasis on literacy and numeracy – and training for work.

As well as research to evaluate the impact of the improved regimes at Holloway and Styal, we have commissioned two further pieces of research which will inform the development of programmes specifically for women. In the past, programmes for women prisoners have been developed on the basis of assumptions about their needs – all too often assumed to be the same as male prisoners rather than facts.

In a *Survey of Women Prisoners' Work Experience and Aspirations,* 600 women have been surveyed and 250 will be followed up post release. This research will inform prisons about how they can develop their regimes to increase the employment options of women on their release, and will also help in the development of more effective regime and resettlement provision generally.

The second piece of research will examine criminogenic factors for women (i.e. the factors that lead to a woman committing a crime) and will be particularly useful in the development of accredited offending behaviour programmes for women. A number of programmes have already been identified for adaptation for women offenders, including Enhanced

Thinking Skills (Foston Hall), a Sex Offender Treatment Programme (Styal), a Young Offender Programme (New Hall), Dialectical Behaviour Therapy (Holloway) and a Problem Solving Programme (Send). A specific Resettlement Programme will also be developed.

In the last few years, there has also been a particular focus on the mixing of different age groups within female establishments. Unlike the male side in which prisoners of different age groups are held separately, female prisons have traditionally catered for all age groups together. We have responded to concerns over this issue by reviewing the policy on age mixing in women's prisons. On 8 March 1999 the Home Secretary announced that with the introduction of the Detention and Training Order, in April 2000, sentenced 15- and 16-year-old girls would be placed in secure accommodation run by local authorities. As spaces become available, sentenced 17-year-old girls are also to move to local authority care. In the interim, girls under 18 years will be held separately from adult prisoners, with other young offenders in more physically discrete accommodation, benefiting from enhanced regimes. Such units have already opened at Holloway and New Hall prisons.

Young offenders

Another group at Prison Headquarters that has been taking forward a programme of extensive change is part of the Government's extensive reform of the youth justice system.

Underpinning the changes in the youth justice system are three principles:

• that the principal aim of the youth justice system is the prevention of offending;

• that the prevention of offending depends critically upon effective inter-agency co-operation and partnership; and

• that work to prevent young people from offending must be evidence-based, that is established on what research has shown really works.

To the Prison Service the programme of change, introduced largely through the Crime and Disorder Act 1998, presents a great challenge and new opportunities. Preparations are well advanced in three areas which will implement the change:

- the holding of almost all boys under 18 years old in facilities separate from other young and adult offenders;

- the construction of new regimes to run in this separate accommodation designed to identify each young person's needs, abilities and aptitudes;

- the development of arrangements, most importantly, high-quality throughcare practice, to enable the successful introduction of a completely new type of custodial sentence for the under 18s, the Detention and Training Order (DTO) which will be introduced in April 2000.

The real difference which the new arrangements will introduce is founded on the understanding that young people aged under 18 years have largely different needs from older offenders. The greatest challenge for the Prison Service is to change the culture of its establishments for young people from the culture of the 'nick' to one more like a secure college where the primary goal is the acquisition of skills and knowledge and understanding which will prevent the young person from offending.

The new regimes being constructed in establishments for under-18-year-olds will be founded on these key features:

- the importance of the **role of staff**: the influential relationships 'significant adults' can positively establish with young people must critically inform the work of staff and the culture of the establishment;

- enabling **personal development**: young people are, by definition, in a developmental phase of their lives. Their physical, emotional, social and health development will be provided for;

- maintaining a **safe and secure environment**: without feeling safe, and with bullying, a common problem young people experience in institutions, young people's development will be inhibited;

- **preventing reoffending**: evidence-based practice now gives confidence that programmes to tackle offending behaviour are truly effective.

Vulnerable prisoners

There are occasions when it is imperative that inmates of Prison Service establishments are segregated from other prisoners. It may be that the nature of their offence, or something they have done while in prison, means that they could be subject to threats, intimidation or attack by other inmates. It is, therefore, desirable in these cases to limit the possibility of injury to the prisoner.

Governors of prisons have powers to remove prisoners from contact with the normal population, under Prison Rule 45. These powers are limited in the time a prisoner can be segregated. However, they can be extended on the authority of a member of the prison's Board of Visitors or the Area Manager.

Once the Governor, and later the Board of Visitors, has accepted that a prisoner needs to be placed on Rule 45, the aim of all concerned should be to assist an early return to normal prison life. The longer the prisoner stays on Rule 45 the more difficult it becomes for him to return. In this, the efforts of the officers who are in regular day-to-day contact with the prisoner are essential. They must get to know the prisoner, gain his confidence and earn his respect. Although many prisoners may despise sex offenders and abusers of children and old people, only a limited number are likely to carry their feelings to the point of physical aggression. Prisoners who have sought protection will often be more readily persuaded that they can return to normal location without fear of injury if they know that it is local management's policy to control potential aggressors.

If this fails, the Prison Service has specialized accommodation known as Vulnerable Prisoner Units. These units allow prisoners who have a similar need for protection to be housed in discrete, self-contained units, providing them with good-quality regimes. The controls placed on Rule 45 prisoners are unnecessary in these units. The prisoners have association with each other within the units and do not suffer deprivation as a result of their separation from the rest of the population.

It is possible to regard vulnerable prisoners simply as a distinctive section of the prison population, who need to be kept separate from other prisoners. The Vulnerable Prisoner Units are housing increasing numbers of sex offenders and these pose a difficult challenge. A large number of units now offer the Sex Offender Treatment Programmes already described.

Conclusion

In this chapter I have tried to give a short review of the developments of constructive regimes in the Prison Service with a focus on some vulnerable prisoners. Having started with a quotation from the Home Secretary, let me end with a quotation from Archbishop William Temple, who summed up the true purpose of constructive regimes in prisons, when he said in 1934, 'We are not what we appear, but what we are becoming; and if that is what we truly are, no penal system is fully just which treats us as anything else'.[2]

II

Aspects of Vulnerability

3

Children in Prison

Compounding Vulnerability

Fran Russell

Over the past six years the number of children (under 18)[1] being sent to prison has nearly doubled and the number of young adults (18–21) has increased by 72 per cent.[2] This is not because offending by young people has increased so dramatically but because a climate has been created, largely by the media and politicians, where children are more feared and demonized than ever before. There is a perception by the courts that the public is clamouring for ever more punitive sentences, and so they oblige.

At any one time there are approximately 2,700 children and 9,800 young adults in prison. Around 3,000 of those will be on remand, the rest convicted of a range of offences from shoplifting to murder. With only around 80 girls and 280 young women in the system, the majority are boys.[3]

Convictions are mainly for theft, burglary and handling stolen goods with a smaller number of convictions for drugs, driving and sex offences. Around 26 per cent have been convicted of violence and robbery.[4]

One overwhelming fact is that whilst prison might prevent offending during the young person's incarceration, it largely fails to prevent future offending. Ninety per cent of 15- to 17-year-old boys released from Young Offenders Institutions are convicted of another offence within two years.[5]

Children in prison – a profile

Children and young people in prison have a range of difficult problems. Despite the bravado they sometimes display they are not, as the media would have us believe, 'bad kids' who have simply chosen in a cold and rational way to 'cock a snoop at society'. Instead, they are vulnerable youngsters, caught in a confusing and unsettling time, stuck between childhood and adulthood, often with a plethora of difficulties of a kind most people would never have to deal with.[6]

Studies have found numerous common background factors which play a part in the lives of children who offend. These include:

- physical, sexual and emotional abuse;

- loss of a significant person such as a parent or grandparent;

- unstable living conditions;

- drug and alcohol abuse;

- inadequate parenting;

- lack of training and employment;

- peer-group pressure;

- aggressive and hyperactive behaviour in early childhood;

- boys are more likely to offend than girls.[7]

Studies show that a staggering number have been in local authority care. The Howard League's reports *Lost Inside*, *Troubleshooter Report*, and *Sentenced to Fail* have found that between 30 and 50 per cent have been in local authority care. The Chief Inspector of Prisons study[8] found 40 per cent of juveniles in prison had such a history.

There is also increasing awareness that many young people in prison are suffering mental illness. Over 50 per cent of remanded and over 30 per cent of sentenced young males have a diagnosable mental disorder.[9]

Dan was physically big, even intimidating, but had a child-like view of life which revolved around clothes, music and attending raves. As we got to know him well it became clear that he spent much of his time in a fantasy world. Unable to read he would spend hours studying the pictures in fashion and music magazines.

His behaviour was bizarre, violent, unpredictable and dangerous. Because of the nature of his offences it was impossible to find a bed in local authority accommodation or to generate much sympathy for his case amongst his local social service and youth justice team. He remained in Feltham for 17 months.

The turning-point came for Dan when a psychometric test carried out at our instigation showed him to have an IQ of 47. This suggested a significant mental impairment which had never previously been picked up. Further inquiry suggested it was possibly because of physical damage to the brain when he was 9. It is a mystery why this profound disability had not been spotted in the educational system as Dan had been a regular attender until the age of 12 and was not 'statemented' by the local authority as being a child with special needs.[10]

Exclusion, truancy and poor educational achievement are startlingly common factors. In a study undertaken by the Howard League,[11] 73 per cent of the group interviewed had been out of school at the date they were sentenced to custody. Many had difficulty reading, with 24 per cent reporting they had been diagnosed as being dyslexic or having other learning difficulties. This coincides with statistics from the Basic Skills Agency which found that between 60 and 70 per cent of the prison population have literacy and numeracy levels so low that they are ineligible for 96 per cent of jobs.

Problems with drugs and alcohol are also common amongst young people in prisons. In the Chief Inspector's study[12] almost two-thirds of those interviewed admitted to misusing drugs at some time in their lives. Almost a quarter had been under the influence of alcohol at the time of their offence. Up to a quarter claimed a current or past drink problem.

Race

A disproportionate number of black and Asian young people are sent to prison. Whereas only 5.5 per cent of the general population are black and Asian, in a study carried out at Feltham YOI,[13] 34 per cent of the boys were black or Asian. Another study of teenage girls in prison[14] found that 18 per cent were black (there were no Asian girls).

In the Feltham study, the numbers were particularly high for those on remand with 45 per cent of the boys being black or Asian. However, the figure drops to 26 per cent for those who were sentenced. Although this is still a disproportionate number, the drop from those remanded is dramatic and suggests that black and Asian youngsters are more likely to be inappropriately remanded than white young people.

What the children want

It is our experience that, whilst on the surface children in prison appear antagonistic to society, underneath there is often a desire to be part of the community. However, they often have no concept of how to achieve this, particularly if they come from a family which is largely excluded from mainstream society.

In the Howard League study *Sentenced to Fail*, 66 young people who had served sentences in Feltham Young Offenders Institution were asked what they wanted for the future. Their answers focused on things that would bring stability to their lives, such as finding a job along with re-entering the education system and finding a home of their own.

Sadly, these aims are much less achievable after serving a custodial sentence. Work is more difficult to obtain and there is evidence that colleges are not always sympathetic to young people who have 'done time'. Some college application forms ask for details of convictions and we understand that a criminal record could be a reason for rejection.

Housing would also seem to be more difficult to find following custody. The *Sentenced to Fail* study found that whilst 4.5 per cent of the group of under 18s interviewed were homeless before prison, 18 per cent were homeless following release.

Exacerbating these problems is the trauma of prison itself (described in the next section). We believe children emerge from prison more damaged, with more problems than before serving their sentence, making long-term rehabilitation all the more difficult.

Jason was a very immature 15-year-old who was identified as being particularly vulnerable to bullying and at risk of self-harm on arrival at Feltham. He had been excluded from school for some 12 months and was in the process of being 'statemented' as he had severe learning difficulties. Living in local authority accommodation at the time of his arrest, he was a heavy user of drugs, particularly amphetamine sulphate.

On arriving at Feltham, Jason was easy to engage in discussion and was open and talkative when first visited. As time went by, he became immersed in the aggressive, macho culture of one group on the remand unit and became less receptive, and even hostile to outside contact. In all, he was held on remand for 4 months on a charge to which he pleaded guilty, and for which he eventually received a 2-year supervision order. In that time the deterioration in his attitude and behaviour was dramatic, as under the influence of older and more sophisticated prisoners, he adapted in order to survive the mayhem of the remand regime. The hardened and manipulative young person who left custody presented a far more difficult proposition to those working with him on supervision, than the damaged child who went in.[15]

Incarcerating children and young people

Young Offenders Institutions

Conditions and regimes

The bulk of young people held in custody are those aged 15 to 21 and are held in Young Offenders Institutions (YOIs) run by the Prison Service. In reality these institutions are prisons. Staffed by prison officers with little or no training in how to deal with adolescents, the regimes, rules, conditions and culture are almost identical to those found in adult jails.

In 1997 the Chief Inspector of Prisons, Sir David Ramsbotham, undertook a thematic review of the way YOIs were run.[16] He found inadequate opportunities for education and work, with 'too many young people confined to their cells for unacceptably long periods of time'.

Of the under 18s he said:

> It is the plight of children that alarms us most, not least because of the conditions in which they are held in prison service accommodation . . . More damage is done to immature adolescents than to any other type of prisoner by current conditions. The vast majority of young people in custody need individual attention given to the problems which produced their criminal behaviour. If all they get is akin to being stored in a warehouse, then the chances of their reoffending, creating yet more victims, is very great.

Some YOIs provide better regimes than others, with opportunities for education and training for some of the young people in their care, but it is not unusual to find youngsters locked in cells for 20 or 23 hours per day with nothing to do. This is particularly the case if they are held on remand. The Chief Inspector found that only in a minority of cases was education provision sufficient and, whilst the quality of individual lessons seen by the Inspectorate was good, on the whole 'such opportunities were not available to the majority of children and young adults'.[17]

The Audit Commission[18] found that young people who truant or are excluded from school are more likely to offend. Education should therefore be a crucial part of a young person's care in prison, particularly since the children have usually had a poor experience of education in the past. In prison they are often more enthusiastic about attending education – an opportunity which should not be missed.

Bullying

In 1997, Sir William Utting wrote in his report *People Like Us* about the need to have safeguards for children living away from home:

> Prison is not a safe environment . . . The review was particularly concerned by the prevalence of bullying ranging from physical brutality to verbal intimidation, in spite of Prison Service strategies for countering it.

The Howard League believes that the ethos of prison exacerbates bullying and that anti-bullying strategies can have only a limited impact. Part of the problem is that, whilst there are staff in prisons who are very talented and extremely committed to working with difficult children and young people, many are totally unsuited to the job. They can themselves unwittingly become bullies and do a great deal of damage.

A young man aged 16 recently interviewed by the Howard League told us:

> The minute you walked into [x YOI] they stripped you of your confidence, everything is taken from you . . . You'd just be walking past an officer and he'd say 'You're a f****** little w*****[19], aren't you?' You would have to answer – 'Yes, sir'.

Bullying is also inevitable if you herd together such a large number of damaged young people and give them little to do.

Drugs

The young man mentioned above also told us that drugs were easily available in prison. This supports our experience generally of all prisons, not just YOIs. It is widely accepted that all kinds of drugs, from cannabis to heroin and crack cocaine, are easily available to young people in prison.

Self-harm and suicide

Given the culture of prison and the plethora of problems the children bring with them, it is not surprising that self-harm and suicide are problems.

Between 1988 and 1998 ninety-nine young people under the age of 21 killed themselves in English and Welsh prisons. Sixteen were under the age of 18.[20]

Accurate figures on the level of self-harm are hard to establish. Between 1994 and 1997 there were 4,212 incidents of self-harm recorded by the Prison Service.[21] However, this does not include prisons holding those remanded and recently sentenced who are the most vulnerable to self-harm and suicide. It is also our understanding that many self-harm incidents go unrecorded because there are so many of them.

What is clear is that young people are particularly at risk of harming themselves in the prison environment.

An end to the imprisonment of children

In his Thematic Review, Sir David Ramsbotham recommended that the Prison Service should no longer be responsible for the care of children (those aged under 18) and that a separate framework should be created. This is a view long espoused by the Howard League and others concerned with children in prison. We do not believe that the Prison Service can provide appropriate environments in which to hold children. Reports damning the quality of care of children and young people in prison have been numerous over many years, yet little fundamental improvement has been made to conditions and treatment.

Feltham Young Offenders Institution is an example. In 1988, the Chief Inspector of Prisons concluded in his report that 'the poor regime at Feltham is unacceptable' (para 4.07). In 1991 a further report stated that 'the regime had developed little and that there appeared to be an over-reliance on the use of control and restraint techniques'.

In 1993, the then Chief Inspector of Prisons, Sir Stephen Tumim, concluded that:

> The treatment of young remands and offenders still gave cause for concern. The basic lifestyle particularly for those in lower levels was unsatisfactory. Many inmates spent too much time in cells which were barren of furniture and devoid of stimulation on first arrival.

In March 1999, during an unannounced inspection of Feltham, Sir David Ramsbotham found children and young adults held 23 hours a day in cold, dirty and dilapidated cells with bed linen unwashed and in a poor state of repair. He described the conditions as 'unacceptable in a civilised society'.

Sir David had made 187 recommendations on how the prison could be improved in his previous report in 1997. On his return, he found a 'marked deterioration' in the provision of care.

It would seem that despite these failings being brought to the attention of the Government and the Prison Service time and time again, little changes, and children remain vulnerable within the walls of Feltham and other Young Offenders Institutions. More disturbing is the fact that in response to Sir David's report, the Prison Service announced plans to take some young men out of Feltham and put them in Chelmsford adult prison. In the Howard League's view this is an even worse setting.

SECURE TRAINING CENTRES

Until March 1998, children under the age of 15 could only be given a custodial sentence if they were convicted of a 'grave offence' (an offence warranting custody of two years or more). However, in March 1998 the Government implemented the new Secure Training Order. This enabled the courts to pass a custodial sentence on 12- to 14-year-old 'persistent offenders', defined as children who have committed three imprisonable offences and been in breach of a supervision order. The sentence lasts for a minimum of four months and a maximum of two years, with half the sentence being spent in a secure training centre and half in the community.[22]

The first secure training centre (STC) opened in April 1998 in Medway, Kent. It is run by Rebound ECD, a wholly owned subsidiary of Group 4, and represents the first child institution to be run by a private company.

In January 1999, the Social Services Inspectorate published a highly critical inspection report. It found that the children had been subjected to excessive use of force and ineffective treatment. It concluded that these factors 'seemed to strengthen the criminogenic behaviours and outlook of the trainees'.

The Inspection team also found:

- unsatisfactory educational provision;

- inadequate numbers of staff;

- inexperienced and incompetent staff who had not been adequately trained;

- lack of effective and experienced managers;

- programmes designed to tackle offending behaviour had 'simply failed';

- some children had virtually no access to fresh air and exercise, leaving them in an enclosed environment for 24 hours a day.

The inspection team highlighted a lack of management. Junior and inexperienced staff worked on the units alone with no one easily available to direct or support them. The centre was short of an essential management tier. The Howard League believes that the reason for this was to save on costs and demonstrates why the private sector is not suited to running institutions for damaged children. The primary purpose of a private company is to improve profits and so increase dividends for their shareholders. This is incompatible with ensuring that the needs of children are met.

The Government announced that an action plan had been agreed with Group 4, but we are not confident that Medway will improve in the long term. Nor are we convinced that the additional four centres planned to open over the next two years will serve any better.

LOCAL AUTHORITY SECURE UNITS

Children who have committed more serious offences, for which the court gives custody for two years or more, are sentenced under section 53 of the Children and Young Persons Act 1933, and if under 15 are held in local authority secure accommodation units. Those aged 15 and over may be held in these units but increasingly they are being incarcerated in Young Offenders Institutions.

Local authority secure accommodation units are child-centred and are run very differently from Young Offenders Institutions. The staff-to-child-ratio is considerably higher and in the good units staff work consistently and constructively with the children, dealing with their needs and challenging behaviour in whatever they are doing during the day, as a good parent would do. They are able to provide specialist help where it is needed, for example in remedial teaching or bereavement counselling.

The cost is considerably higher than with Young Offenders Institutions at around £3,000 per week per child, and the centres are not always perfect. There are poorly run secure units which are every bit as damaging as a prison, but in principle, where a child genuinely needs a secure environment we believe this kind of child-centred institution is the most appropriate.

Government changes

A new sentence of a Detention and Training Order (DTO) was introduced in April 1999, creating one sentence for all 10- to 18-year-olds, although the sentence for 'grave offences' providing custody for two years or more will remain.

Under the new provisions the Government is creating a secure estate for juveniles encompassing all the institutions at present available for this age group – YOIs, STCs, local authority accommodation units, and the Youth Treatment Centre which takes particularly vulnerable children. Children sentenced to a DTO will be held in any one of these institutions.

To coincide with this change, due to be implemented in April 2000, will be the creation of the Youth Justice Board (YJB) whose purpose will be to oversee the whole provision of youth justice including administering the secure estate. It will have a purchasing role, buying beds from the various institutions to hold the children similar to the internal market existing in the NHS.

In response to these changes, the Prison Service is designating institutions where juveniles will be held and is developing a 'juvenile regime' for which the Government has also provided some extra money. However, we are not confident of a positive outcome, given the past experience which has shown us that the Prison Service is not able to improve conditions sufficiently for children. We are doubtful that the 'internal market' will work to push up standards since pressure of numbers will mean that the YJB will have no choice but to use Prison Service YOIs, even if they are not of an acceptable standard.

Conclusion

We believe that the best way of protecting children and young people from the damage done by prison is not to send them there in the first place. For this reason we support Sir David Ramsbotham's call for the Prison Service to relinquish all responsibility for the under 18s.

The use of custody needs to be reduced. The huge increase in the use of custody in recent years in itself indicates that custody is being overused.

We accept that some children will need to be held in secure environments but believe these should be small units, with a child-centred approach. We do not believe that the private sector should be involved in such provision as their need to maximize profit interferes with the need to provide quality care as a first priority.

However, to reduce the use of custody we must change attitudes. It is crucial to persuade the public and sentencers that children who commit crime are intrinsically vulnerable and that their status as children is not relinquished by virtue of their having committed a crime, no matter how serious. The way in which we hold children in prison reflects badly on our society. It is time it stopped.

4

Women in Prison

Victims Yet Again

Clare Sparks

Some people – some prison reformers even – base their compassion for prisoners on a 'There but for the grace of God, go I' principle. And it is true that many of us have either broken the law or been tempted to do so. But those who are caught and punished are not, in the main, drawn from nice middle-class suburbs. They are the dispossessed. The underclass. The socially excluded.

In the case of women prisoners, they are the people described in a recent Home Office study:

> The women in this sample were broadly typical . . . of female prisoners elsewhere. They were generally young, criminally unsophisticated, and were mainly in prison for property offences. Over 40 per cent were mothers of dependent children and nearly half these mothers were single parents. Nearly 60 per cent of the women said that they were living solely on benefits prior to their imprisonment . . . Almost a half of the women reported having used drugs prior to their imprisonment and more than half of these women associated their offending with their drug use.
>
> Nearly one quarter of the women reported harming themselves either by slashing/cutting or by attempting suicide prior to their imprisonment . . . more than half the

women had not expected a prison sentence and more than
two thirds had never been in prison before . . . nearly half the
women reported having been physically abused and nearly
one third reported having been sexually abused.[1]

Vulnerability, exclusion and alienation are the experiences of most people
in prison. These themes have a special resonance for the 3,200 women and
girls currently imprisoned in England and Wales. This is a group whose
members are vulnerable as individuals damaged by their life experience,
but also as a minority within the wider (predominantly male) prison system.

Prison staff have told me that working with women in prison is a
complete contrast to working with men. Women respond to imprisonment differently to men – intellectually, physically, emotionally and
behaviourally. Staff say that women are 'always in your face', that they are
'always asking questions'. Women 'bring the family and home into prison
with them, and do not leave the outside world outside'.

As individuals, the personal vulnerability of women in prison can usually
be tracked through a history of local authority care, low educational
attainment, exclusion from school, physical and sexual abuse and drug
use. A recent survey carried out by the Office for National Statistics[2]
reported that 48 per cent of the sentenced female prison population had
experienced violence at home, a quarter had experienced bullying and a
further 31 per cent had experienced sexual abuse. These findings reflect
other studies. A review by Sir David Ramsbotham, the indefatigable Chief
Inspector of Prisons,[3] reports that nearly half the women interviewed had
been abused. A third of these reported both physical and sexual abuse, a
third said they had been sexually abused and the remainder reported
physical abuse. The same study reported that 36 per cent of the women
reported having had serious problems at school and as many as 70 per
cent said they had had no previous employment before coming to prison.
Over 40 per cent of the women interviewed reported that they had
harmed themselves intentionally and/or attempted suicide. The reasons
ranged from histories of physical and/or sexual abuse, family and
relationship problems, depression and stress.

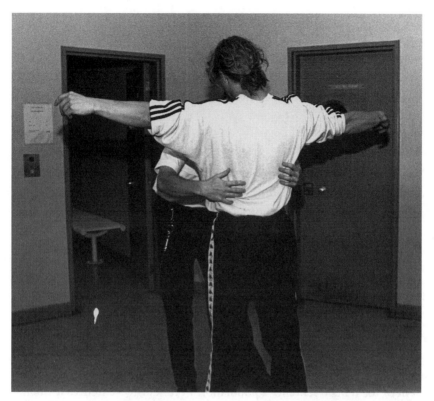

Plate 2:   Women are searched when they are admitted to prison; drug searches may also be common. *Jason Shenai, for the Prison Reform Trust.*

But despite the distinctive and pressing needs of women prisoners, it was only in April 1998 that the Prison Service established a Women's Policy Group at Prison Service Headquarters. Up until that point, policy affecting women had been dealt with together with policy affecting young offenders. It is the first time in 25 years that specific provision has been made to consider the issues facing women's prisons and women prisoners.

While the creation of the Women's Policy Group has been widely welcomed, and the Group has pushed ahead with an impressive programme of work, there are doubts about its real impact. The Group has no operational responsibility or line management contact with the women's prisons. Nor does it have a ringfenced budget. The creation of the

Women's Policy Group has been a significant move in terms of acknowledging the different needs of women in prison, but there remains a question as to its impact on practice. Some Prison Governors have told the Prison Reform Trust that the Group has improved communication, but that its effect at establishment level is limited.

Population trends

Most crime is committed by men. Few, if any, people are frightened of leaving home for fear of meeting a female offender. Most offending by women involves property, not violence. It therefore comes as a surprise to most people to learn that the women's prison population has more than doubled in the last six years. Indeed while the male prison population rose by 60 per cent between 1992 and 1998, the percentage rise for the women's population was 133 per cent.[4] The women's population passed the 3,000 mark at the end of 1998 for the first time since 1904 and now stands at 3,217 (12 March 1999).[5]

There are two ways of looking at the prison population. One is to take a 'snapshot' to see who is there on a particular day. In mid-1997, 37 per cent of the female sentenced population were serving sentences for drugs offences, a further 24 per cent for theft and fraud. Just under 20 per cent were imprisoned for violence or sexual offences. Of the remainder, 5 per cent were imprisoned for robbery, 5 per cent for burglary and 10 per cent for 'other' offences. The main changes over the last decade have been that the proportion serving sentences for violent and drug offences has increased while the proportion serving sentences for theft and fraud has decreased.[6]

With regard to sentence length, over three-quarters of adult females received sentences of twelve months or less, a further 19 per cent had sentences of over twelve months and up to four years and 5 per cent had sentences of four years or more.[7]

The other way to look at the prison population is to consider throughput. These statistics better reflect the high incidence of women serving short sentences for property crimes. Of the 3,994 women who were received into Prison Service custody during 1997, 38 per cent were imprisoned for theft and handling offences. A further 16 per cent were imprisoned for drug offences, 11 per cent for violence or sexual offences, 9 per cent for fraud, 3 per cent for burglary and 1.5 per cent for robbery. Of the remainder, 17 per cent were serving sentences for 'other' crimes – mainly driving under the influence of drink or drugs, or other motoring offences, threatening or disorderly behaviour or breach of a court order. For 3 per cent of women, their offence was not recorded.[8]

This chapter focuses on the vulnerability of women in prison in four specific areas. It considers women on remand, women prisoners with mental health problems, the impact of drugs and women's role as primary carers.

Women on remand

Under the Bail Act 1984 there is a presumption in favour of bail. But there are four primary criteria under which someone can be remanded to custody. These are:

• likelihood of not appearing for trial;

• fear that the defendant will interfere with witnesses;

• to prevent offending;

• for their own protection.

The presumption in favour of bail has been weakened somewhat in recent years, and much attention has been given in the media to so-called 'bail bandits'. Many of us think the criteria should be strengthened. The Prison Reform Trust has argued that consideration should also be given to an individual's physical and mental health in determining whether a custodial remand is appropriate, and to the likelihood of a custodial sentence eventually being imposed.

Between 1996 and 1997, receptions of male and female remand prisoners increased by 7.2 per cent. The average remand population in 1997 was

12,100; women accounted for 4.9 per cent (612 women), continuing the gradual increase which started in 1993. Those held on remand in 1997 made up one-quarter of the total population of women in prison. Of these, nearly a quarter were acquitted, a further 45 per cent were either discharged, fined or given a community penalty, while only 30 per cent were sentenced to immediate custody following a finding of guilt.[9]

Yet even a very short remand to custody can have a significant impact. Women I have interviewed report going to court without being aware that custodial remand was a possibility, leaving young children with a friend or neighbour and not returning. The personal distress that this causes to many women, alongside the experience of unexpected imprisonment and the humiliation of the reception procedure – characterized as 'strip and twirl' – is very real.

Considering that only a quarter of those women remanded to custody will receive a custodial sentence, there is an overwhelming argument for saying that custodial remand is used unnecessarily. There is a lack of proper research on why magistrates remand women who will not in the end receive a custodial sentence. However, there is some anecdotal evidence. One suggestion is that there is what might be termed a 'demonization' of women involved in crime. For a woman to appear in court she must have been 'really bad'. There is also perhaps a perception among magistrates that women who are in court on drug or drug-related charges may be better off in prison, because they will not be able to access any illegal drugs. Sadly this is not the case. A third explanation is that if magistrates suspect a woman will get a community penalty on sentence, then some believe a few days on remand in prison will give her a 'short sharp shock' and deter her from further involvement in crime.

Whether all these explanations together provide a coherent picture of why so many women are inappropriately remanded is debatable. But the simple fact that only a quarter of women remanded to custody will eventually receive a custodial sentence is nothing short of a scandal. Bail Information Schemes in some women's prisons have attempted to provide courts with clear alternatives to the custodial remand. HMP Holloway, for example, receives women remanded from all the London courts. Staff say that many are only remanded for three or four days. Many are very vulnerable women; for some it will be their first experience of custody. The Holloway Bail Information Scheme provides an alternative to a custodial remand. The team puts together an action plan for the woman to present at her next court hearing – perhaps including residence at a bail hostel, opportunities for contact with children or contact with a drug treatment agency.

Women prisoners with mental health problems

Mentally disordered women in prison are perhaps the most difficult and vulnerable group within the system. The very fact of being sent to prison can exacerbate their condition.

The Office for National Statistics has found that 40 per cent of women prisoners reported receiving help or treatment for a mental, nervous or emotional problem in the year before they came to prison. One in five women on remand had been admitted to a mental hospital or ward at some time in their lives. The rate was slightly lower for sentenced women. Half the women assessed in detail in the survey had at least one type of personality disorder – 14 per cent of women were assessed as having a functional psychosis, most of which were schizophrenia and delusional disorders. One in ten had self-harmed during their current prison term. Nearly two in five women reported having attempted suicide at some time in their life.[10]

These stark statistics attempt to describe women with a wide range of psychiatric disorders. The women who are housed on C1 Wing at Holloway Prison include some awaiting transfer to a special (psychiatric) hospital.

On a recent visit to HMP Holloway, a colleague and I met a woman I will call Sarah. Sarah was on 24-hour suicide watch because she had been trying to kill herself for some days. She was locked in what the Prison Service terms a 'strip cell', that is one without any 'ligature points' – points from which Sarah could attempt to hang herself. There was no furniture in the room apart from a concrete plinth which was Sarah's bed. Even the mattress had been removed because staff were afraid she would try and eat the stuffing to choke herself.

Sarah had all her clothes removed and had been wearing a 'strip gown'. These look like green hospital gowns which fasten at the back using Velcro. However they are made of a special material which cannot be torn up to form a ligature. Sarah had even had this removed from her because she had been rubbing her face raw with the Velcro fastening. She stood alone wrapped in a thin blanket, being watched through the hatch in her door by a nurse.

Sarah should not have been in Holloway. She was due out in a matter of two or three months and it was the prison's priority to keep her alive until she left. The Senior Medical Officer was working to get Sarah placed in a Special Hospital where she could receive treatment.

Prisoners like Sarah demand a tremendous amount of time and resource from healthcare staff. Finding a Special Hospital place can be particularly time-consuming. But prisons do not always deal sensitively with women's behaviour. Those assessed as having a personality disorder are more likely to report being held in cellular confinement, being given added days (loss of remission) and being held in stripped conditions.

There are also women with a range of lesser psychiatric disorders for whom there is still a pressing need for treatment. The Prison Service aims 'To give prisoners access to the same quality and range of health care services as the general public receives from the National Health Service'.[11] But in practice, psychiatric services for women with mental health problems of a less severe nature are limited. Different prisons offer varying degrees of psychiatric input. Officer staff, who deal with women on a day-to-day basis, are poorly trained to recognize and deal with the issues that arise.

Drugs

The issues of drug treatment and control are high on the agenda in British prisons. Recent statistics show that half of women received into prison have a drug-related offence on their charge sheet. This does not include those women whose offending is of an acquisitive nature, but is linked to a drug habit. One Governor of a women's prison told me that her own survey had shown that 76 per cent of the women received had a heroin addiction.

The Prison Service has a Drugs Strategy which has a three-strand approach to dealing with drugs in prison:

- reducing the supply of drugs;

- reducing the demand for drugs in prison and rehabilitating drug misusers;

- measures to reduce the potential for damage to the health of prisoners, staff and the wider community, arising from the misuse of drugs.[12]

Reducing the supply of drugs to prisons is the aspect of the strategy which has received the most attention through the introduction of tougher security measures, random drug testing, sniffer dogs, high-tech CCTV during visits and increased use of closed visits for family and friends.

So far as treatment is concerned, the Prison Service aims to ' . . . provide clinical services for the assessment, treatment and care of substance misusers comparable to those available in the community and appropriate to the prison setting'.[13]

But while good programmes have been established at some men's prisons, the picture within the women's estate is far from satisfactory. Additional resources from the Government's Comprehensive Spending Review have allowed some women's prisons to bid for money to provide suitable treatment programmes. This is not a moment too soon.

Prison provides a rare opportunity to help women with drug problems. But there is not much point having a drug-free prison (not that we enjoy such a luxury) if women return to drug use immediately on release. Services for drug-using offenders in prison should be integrated with services for women in the community. Only too often women are detoxed in prison and after a short sentence return to the community with no support to continue in treatment. Indeed there are stories of women overdosing on release, not realizing that their body has lost its tolerance of drugs during their time inside.

Women as primary carers

Imprisonment is a family experience whatever the gender of the prisoner. As the Prison Service itself has acknowledged:

> The disruption of the inmate's position within the family unit represents one of the most distressing aspects of imprison-ment . . . the nature of a prisoner's relationships with his or her family will be an important factor in determining whether he or she will succeed in leading a useful and law-abiding life on return to the community.[14]

But the problem is most acute for women. Time and again, women say that the most difficult part of the prison sentence is lack of contact with, and information about, what is going on in the family at home. A study of mothers in prison, conducted in 1994 by the Home Office Research and Planning Unit, reported that of the 1,766 women who were interviewed, 43 per cent had dependent children.[15] More recent research carried out by the Prison Inspectorate in 1997 found higher rates, with nearly two-thirds of its sample having at least one child under the age of 16. On average the women had three children.

Just a quarter of the children whose mothers were in prison were being cared for by their biological father or their mother's current partner. In contrast, a survey of male prisoners has shown that over 90 per cent of their children were being looked after by their mother or the man's current partner. Women tend to rely on their own mothers (27 per cent) or family/friends (29 per cent). Around ten per cent had their children placed in local authority care, fostered or adopted.[16]

A few of the women's prisons have schemes which provide an opportunity for children to spend 'quality time' with their mother for the whole day. Styal Prison runs all-day children's visits. A carer brings the child to the prison in the morning and leaves them to spend the day with their mother. Parents and children can make use of the various facilities in prison including specially provided toys. Mothers are able to cook for their children and eat lunch with them. They spend the afternoon together until the carer comes to collect the child at the end of the day. These schemes are greatly appreciated by the women and by their children. But one difficulty is women's reliance on others to bring the child. This is a particular issue if family members have to travel a significant distance and then have to wait around to collect the child later on. If the child is being looked after by Social Services the difficulties are exacerbated. Women are sometimes told that visits cannot be continued because they cannot be funded by the local authority.

The simple fact is that there are only about 16 prisons for women in England and Wales in comparison to around 125 prisons for men (a few of the male prisons have female wings). The result is that women are likely to be housed at much greater distances from home than men, placing significant pressure on women and their families in maintaining good quality relationships.

Foreign national prisoners, who make up 10 per cent of the women's population, face particular difficulties in making contact with home. Many serve very long sentences for charges of drug importation and can have no contact with their families throughout that time. Some prisons try to promote family contact for foreign nationals. Winchester Prison allows foreign nationals a five-minute telephone call once a month in lieu of visits.

For all women prisoners, their role as primary carers is an example of the differential impact that imprisonment has on women compared with men. The social costs of their imprisonment echo down the years. It is said that on a recent visit to a mother-and-baby unit in one prison, a Government Minister came face to face with a mother who had herself been born in the unit 20 years earlier.

What is to be done?

In a recent ground-breaking report on women's imprisonment in Scotland, HM Chief Inspector of Prisons for Scotland quoted in his preface the view of the Prison Reform Trust that the number of women prisoners who actually pose a grave danger to the general public can be counted on the fingers of one hand.[17] Far from being a threat to the public, many of these women are in fact damaged, vulnerable and indeed more of a danger to themselves than to society at large.

Quite simply many, and perhaps most, should not be there at all. Custodial remands should be the exception, not the rule. Custodial sentences should be as short as possible.

We should not consider the walls of prisons as a barrier. Rather, prison walls are permeable, with people going into prison and re-entering society every day. Most women in custody will shortly return to the community. Services need to reflect that reality, providing effective follow-through and resettlement plans after release.

Prison is a bad place for anyone. It is a bad bargain for the taxpayer. A bad working place for prison staff. And, all too often, a deeply damaging experience for prisoners.

Perhaps it is in the nature of the prison to be beyond reform. Perhaps the very practice of separating the offender from her community ties necessarily outweighs any possible benefit from constructive regimes.

Certainly the number of women prisoners could and should be reduced drastically. (In the 1960s, the Government actually expected women's imprisonment to disappear like earlier social ills such as slavery or cholera.) For the women prisoners who remain, we need much smaller institutions, much more community-based, and staffed and resourced to combat the manifold personal and social disadvantage to which women prisoners are subject.

Where are you now, Elizabeth Fry?

5

Mentally Disordered Offenders

A Psychiatric Perspective

Ian Cummings

The portrayal of the mentally ill offender is not a kind one. Those in prison are drawn into the general debate that society explores from time to time when a crime (and usually a serious one) is committed by mentally ill people. With predictability they are seen as a casual phenomenon of prison life. In the same way that society seeks to draw its boundaries between those who are in prison and those who are not, so mentally ill people in prison are cut off from the processes and systems available to those who are similarly ill in the wider community. For some offenders it is the first time that they may be identified as being mentally ill. For others there is an endless round between prison, hospital and community. As we shall see, there are many obstacles ahead of those in need of treatment, not least of which are the legal structures into which mentally ill people often fit clumsily.

There are a number of obvious questions to ask:

1. How many mentally disordered offenders are in prison?

2. Why are mentally ill people in prison?

3. Should they be there and what risks does prison pose to such individuals?

4. What can be done and what is being done to address these issues?

Mentally ill people have always been associated with prison and, no doubt, always will. Even from the earliest days, prison surprisingly attempted both to highlight and to address the problem. Prisons have not always had the perfunctory role that is now associated with them. They have been places of correction as well as simple incarceration. In the past, solitary confinement and silence were enforced. The Medical Officer in 1852, Dr William Baly, recognized that such regimes could have a detrimental effect on prisoners. Later he made arrangements to allow the association of prisoners who were 'mentally infirm'. The Prison Hulks, which had been developed to act as a temporary confinement site for those to be transported, were perhaps the first areas within the Prison System where those who were 'weak minded' were put together. Later, prisons such as Dartmoor and Parkhurst were identified as having a special responsibility for those who were both physically and mentally infirm.

In recent decades, researchers have tried to quantify the problem. A study by Maden *et al.*[1] on remand prisoners found overall rates of psychosis of 5.9 per cent. A previous study by Gunn *et al.*[2] of sentenced prisoners detected, as one would expect, lower rates of psychosis of 2.4 per cent for men and 1.1 per cent for women. Comparable studies by Teplin in Chicago[3] found rates of around 6 per cent. More recently the Office of National Statistics (1997) found prevalences of probable psychotic disorder (established through lay interview) of 9 per cent and 4 per cent for remand and sentenced prisoners respectively.[4] Maden *et al.*[5] estimate that the implications are that around 5 per cent of the remand population will need to be transferred out to appropriate psychiatric hospitals under the Mental Health Act for psychosis alone. This should not mislead us into ignoring the much higher figures of other mental disorders such as neurotic disorder, alcohol and drug problems and, of course, personality disorder. The same study by Maden *et al.*[6] described the following results in addition to those described above:

	Adult Males		Adult Females	
	Sentenced	*Remand*	*Sentenced*	*Remand*
	%	%	%	%
Neurosis	5.2	15	13.2	27.7
Personality Disorder	7.3	9.9	8.4	13.5
Substance Misuse	20.1	28.1	28.9	26.1

Knowing that there are significant numbers of people with mental illness leads us to search for a reason why. This second question is as complicated as the first question is straightforward. Most people would point to the failures of community care and the closure of the asylums. The media are keen to emphasize this side of psychiatric care and forget that mentally ill people have always been associated with prisons and offending, though this has not previously been adequately measured. Stays are shorter in hospital than they have ever been, and many would accuse the services themselves of discharging patients too early. Like other medical colleagues, psychiatrists have finite resources which have increasingly become polarized towards a psychosis-based service. Pressures to admit and provide a bed come from many sources and are frequently needs-driven. The shorter stays result from inadequate resources in the NHS. After discharge they often feel frustrated in trying to stabilize and maintain an individual in the community who chooses to stop his or her medication. Measures have been introduced to formalize monitoring arrangements and identify risk, but these often lack the teeth that are required to prevent relapse. A series of well-publicized cases has gathered momentum with the media and public alike. Because of this hype there is more social and judicial intolerance to allowing individuals with mental illness to be in the community. Those charged with more minor offences are more likely to be given remand into custody rather than bail or even a caution. This is paralleled with an increasing reluctance to take such offenders out of prison by the services themselves, because of such factors as bed availability and future resource implications. Confusion reigns when the diagnosis is less clear-cut, or has an added complication such as drug mis-use or issues related to personality. The mentally ill offender carries a heavy stigma felt by all.

This leads to the next question: should mentally ill offenders be in prison? There seems to be a trend in the profession towards the view that men-tally disordered offenders should be held responsible. Most consultant psychiatrists will know of individuals who endlessly rotate between prison, hospital and non-compliance in the community. Removal from prison is simplistically seen as an escape from responsibility and uncom-fortably challenges their own social mores. In addition they must weigh up the stresses and rigours that prison will exert on their patients. Most would agree that prison should fulfil a number of roles. It must protect society and contain offenders safely for a period. Its other roles are more confusing and divisive. Is containment punishment enough, or should the milieu be such that it will deter future offending? Though there are often cases where the nature of the illness affects responsibility, there are also those where responsibility is far more obvious and professionals and the public are more likely to condone incarceration as punishment than allow an escape from justice. *In my own view*, until prisons can provide or approximate the level of care that is available within the NHS, every effort should be made to divert the mentally ill offender from custody.

Those that work in prisons know the reality bears little resemblance to the media portrayal. Most employees perform a necessary and difficult job, maintaining the balance between custodian and guardian. Scant resources compound the difficulties in achieving an environment where individuals are contained, supported, provided for and given as healthy a lifestyle as possible. Prisons are of course hostile, but for many different reasons. Rules and procedures have become established because of cus-tom or necessity. Escapism through drugs, self-harm and violence produces an antagonistic culture. Into this are stirred mentally ill prison-ers and those with substance misuse problems, learning difficulties and other mental disorders. Psychotic states originating in prison occur with astonishing regularity, and relapses are often precipitated.[7]

The mentally ill offender must steer a difficult and complicated course through the courts, prisons, Mental Health Act and hospitals to finally get the treatment that is needed. Being 'insane' is not enough. Some do not make it and suicide is a sad, albeit infrequent outcome. The Chief Inspector of Prisons, Sir David Ramsbotham, plans to review the suicide prevention policy in prisons throughout England and Wales. The initiative followed news that the number of people taking their own life in British prisons had reached an all-time high. In 1997, 83 people committed suicide in prison, 68 of those in England and Wales. This is several times higher than the rate for males in the general population. Suicide is four times more likely on remand or recently sentenced, than in the rest of the prison population. Though psychiatric illness is an important contributing factor, it is an unfortunate perspective that suicide and its reduction is a reflection of mental health care. Successful suicides are also associated with increased frequency of alcohol misuse, and previous suicide attempts. The effect of the milieu, charge, and removal to unfamiliar surroundings are other potent factors.

Drug misuse is widespread in prisons throughout the world. Though some will turn to drug use for the first time in prison, most have already been users before they arrive. The statistics above indicate the prevalence of substance misuse. As a whole, drug misuse in arrestees is high. Bennett showed with urine testing, that 61 per cent of people arrested had taken at least one illegal drug.[8] Cannabis was found most often, with 46 per cent testing positive for it. Comparatively high proportions of those arrested tested positive for heroin/opiates (18 per cent) and cocaine/crack (10 per cent). In prison, the rates are also higher. A recent study by O'Donnell and Edgar[9] reports that three out of four prisoners had smoked cannabis at some time in prison. Four out of ten had taken heroin or misused prescribed medications. The inmates' self-reports showed that cannabis and heroin are the preferred drugs in prison. Five of the prisoners interviewed (over a quarter of the drug users) said they were introduced to heroin while in custody. Recent introduction of mandatory drug testing (MDT) may have produced some reduction in drug use, but it has also led to a switch from cannabis to heroin because cannabis is more easily detected in the body and for a greater length of time.

One of the most threatening aspects of prison life is the real and perceived violence. O'Donnell and Edgar note that almost one in three young offenders reported being assaulted in the previous month, as did one in five (19 per cent) of the adults.[10] Interviews revealed that assaults were commonly motivated by simple retaliation, the wish to settle a conflict with force, the desire to enhance one's status, the lure of material gain, or to relieve boredom. Not unexpectedly, threats of violence were more common than assaults. About half (44 per cent) of the young offenders and a quarter (26 per cent) of the adults reported having been threatened with violence on at least one occasion in the preceding month.

The psychiatrist in prison straddles a variety of roles and obeys several masters. A man who is obviously psychotic and in need of treatment must wait in custody until he can be given hospital treatment. Compulsory treatment under the Mental Health Act does not apply in prison and any forcible medication is an assault. Conversely, a patient who had been psychotic but was compliant with medication, may then delay his transfer because the improvement has reduced his perceived risk in prison.

Perhaps surprisingly, in terms of the Mental Health Act, there is a variety of different routes out of custody at all stages of the judicial process. Delay in transfer is all too common, and may be due to a combination of factors such as lack of beds (at all levels of security) and issues regarding risk and treatability.

Mentally disordered offenders are not a modern or localized phenomenon. They are intimately associated with prisons, and remain vulnerable in such an environment. Removal is not always the solution. Improving the management of mentally disordered offenders requires a number of changes including alterations in the Mental Health Act, provision of psychiatric care in prisons and the NHS and/or the private sector. Now that the levels of mental disorder are known, effective systems of detection are gradually developing in both the judicial and penal systems. These systems need to be matched by an effective delivery of health care for the mentally disordered offender in both the NHS and prison.

The Prison Service has been subject to many reviews and recommendations over the years to try and improve the delivery of health care. Recently a document has been released to provide a fundamental change in how health care is provisioned and delivered (*The Future Organisation of Prison Health Care*). This document recommends that a formal partnership develop between the NHS and the Prison Service. For mental health there are some important suggestions. These include the recommendation that the care of mentally ill prisoners should develop in line with NHS mental health policy, and that better attention should be paid to screening for mental illness upon reception. These recommendations would seem to represent the beginnings of substantive change in how health care needs are perceived and provided.

Appendix to Chapter 5

In Memory of Christopher Edwards

'A Simple Call for Justice', taken from the *Church Times*

Plate 3: Christopher Edwards, 1964–1994.
Reproduced with the kind permission of his family.

'A Simple Call for Justice'

This essay has been taken from the Church Times, *12 November 1997 and slightly edited to account for the time elapsed.*

In November 1994, Paul and Audrey Edwards took a telephone call from Colchester Police. Their 30-year-old son, Christopher, had been arrested for a minor public-order offence. After a brief court appearance the following morning he was remanded in custody in Chelmsford Prison. Twenty-four hours later he had been kicked to death by his cellmate.

Christopher Edwards was mentally ill, and so was the man who murdered him. Devastated by the manner of his death, Christopher's parents started their own campaign for a complete change in prison culture, and the proper recognition of a duty of care to vulnerable inmates. Above all, they want to see an end to the practice of sending the mentally ill to prison.

When Christopher Edwards was arrested, he had been suffering from mental distress for four years, but was not violent. After a night in a police cell, his mental condition visibly worsened. The police, the court and the prison were fully aware of his condition and medical history.

Richard Linford, who murdered him, suffered from a severe mental disorder, and was known to be so violent that staff in the mental hospital where he spent regular periods were fearful for their own safety. The day he was sent to Chelmsford Prison, three policemen were needed to escort him into court.

Confusion still surrounds the decision to put the two men together in one cell; both men were supposed to be isolated (as initially happened), as a matter of safety. There is uncertainty about whether the cell alarm buzzer was working, and whether Christopher knew of its existence.

The stark facts remain that, at one o'clock in the morning, six prison officers saw Richard Linford stamping on Christopher Edwards. Rather than entering the cell immediately, they left to don riot gear. By the time they came back it was too late. Christopher Edwards had been so brutally injured that he had to be identified by his dental records.

For his parents, the agony had only just begun. It was three-and-a-half months before their son's body was released for burial, and their attempts to discover the truth about the events surrounding his death met obstacles at every turn.

It was the attempt by the police and Prison Service to cover up what had happened to Christopher which destroyed the Edwards' trust in this country's criminal-justice system. 'What happened to Christopher was terrible. What happened afterwards was even worse', says Mrs Edwards.

'We are not seeking vengeance, but we are seeking substantial improvement', Mrs Edwards says. 'We feel we have a moral responsibility to do something about it. Christopher was a devout Christian, and he would have wished, as we do, that the lessons which can be learned from his death might bring life to others.'

The Edwards believe passionately that the mentally ill have no place in prison. 'All of the evidence available to us has strengthened our conviction that it is unchristian and inhumane to send mentally ill people to prison; and yet this continues to happen', says Mrs Edwards. 'A report in the British Medical Journal [in December 1996] shows that around a third of remand prisoners, and a quarter of all prisoners, are mentally ill.'

'I think there was a legitimate reaction against the old asylums', says Mr Edwards. 'But now it's gone too far the other way. Prisons are awful places, and to send someone who is mentally ill into that environment is disastrous. Yet, they are closing mental hospitals and building more prisons all the time.'

Between 70 and 80 people commit suicide in prison every year. 'Sending the mentally ill to prison makes their mental condition worse, and it makes prisons overcrowded and more difficult to manage', says Mr Edwards. 'Some of the billions of pounds currently allocated for building new prisons should be diverted to the provision of secure mental-health facilities, so that mentally ill people can be held in more appropriate facilities.'

But the Edwards believe the entire culture of the criminal-justice system needs changing. 'While there are good and dedicated people working within the police and Prison Service, the prevailing institutional culture, in our experience, is one of disdain verging on contempt for offenders, particularly the mentally ill; and this extends to their families', he says.

'It is a matter of changing people's attitudes. If all the standard recommendations and rules and safeguards had been implemented, Christopher would be alive today.'

They would also like to see increased powers for compulsory hospitalization and medication for the mentally ill. 'Society has a responsibility for its weakest members', he says. 'People unconscious after an accident are not denied medical assistance when they are unable to ask for it; and it should not be denied to the mentally ill, who are unconscious of their condition.'

Christopher never recognized his illness, and was unwilling to seek help; and because he was an adult, Mr and Mrs Edwards found themselves excluded by the medical profession. 'They shut us out', says Mrs Edwards. 'We had no support. It's very characteristic of mental illness not to recognize it. If they had only worked with us, we could have persuaded him to go into hospital for treatment. But their philosophy got in the way.'

Christopher was never formally diagnosed, although his parents are now convinced he suffered from Asperger's Syndrome. He displayed all the characteristics: he was clumsy, lacked self-esteem, could not initiate human contact, struggled to make friendships, would home in on one thing to the point of obsession. An outstanding linguist, he had always been shy; but it was not until his second year at university that the first signs of his illness emerged. 'He was a very gentle person, very loving and devoted. He never heard voices, and he was never violent or rude', say his parents.

His one previous encounter with the criminal-justice system came in 1991. Christopher, whose mother is an Anglican and whose father a Roman Catholic, became obsessed with the idea that he must be confirmed into the Church of England, instantly, 'because he thought he was doomed'. He began to pester the local vicar in Hillingdon, where he was living at the time. On one occasion the vicar – who had been very tolerant – was away, and the curate called the police. When Christopher appeared before the local magistrates, however, the court probation officer persuaded him to plead not guilty, and the case was dropped. 'We did not query this at the time, but in retrospect it was a missed opportunity for Christopher to be required to receive medical attention', say his parents now.

Shortly afterwards, Christopher moved back to the family home in Coggeshall, in Essex, where he transferred his obsession with instant confirmation to the local vicar, who was also very supportive.

Meanwhile, his parents persuaded him to see a psychiatrist, who prescribed medication. 'He never accepted his illness, but he took his medicine to please his mother', says Mr Edwards. With medication, he made some progress, but he refused to go into hospital, and after two visits, chose not to go back to the psychiatrist. His file was closed.

The Edwards believe they were badly let down by the health service. Their local churches (both Anglican and Roman Catholic) have been supportive, however. 'The Christian community, and particularly our vicar, were more helpful to Christopher in his mental distress than the paid professionals', says Mrs Edwards.

They are now calling on the Church as a body to speak out on behalf of the mentally ill and prisoners. 'Five years ago, we didn't think prisons were anything to do with us. In so far as we thought about the criminal-justice system, we would have presumed it to be a fair, socially responsible and appropriately caring structure, and would have thought that prisons were there to accommodate criminals.

'We now realize how unjust the system is. The mentally ill and prisoners are bottom of the pile, with no champions. The Christian thing to do is to express solidarity and support. No one else is going to do it.'

Mr Edwards believes individual Christians must also take responsibility. 'If every Christian person took their Christianity into their job, there would be more care in the criminal-justice system. Where these institutions have become self-protective, Christians need to be prepared to speak out, to make sure that the truth comes first.'

On a local level, the Christian community could support the mentally ill and their families by not avoiding the subject, says Mrs Edwards. 'If only people could say, "I know your son is ill, I acknowledge your pain, and I am suffering with you", that would make a difference. Mental illness is nothing to be ashamed of. I was never ashamed of Christopher.'

Remarkably, perhaps, Christopher Edwards' parents are not bitter. They say their faith has saved them. 'I don't know how people cope without faith', says Mrs Edwards. 'There are times when you feel so weak, you feel you can't go on. Then you pray, and feel the strength return.' She has been in touch with Richard Linford's mother and gathers 'he is doing very well' in a secure mental unit. 'The pain never goes away', she says. 'I do feel anger with the Prison Service, but sorrow more than anything, now.'

Postscript: *The Report of the Inquiry into the Care and Treatment of Christopher Edwards and Richard Linford was published in June 1998. It recognized some of the failures of the Prison Service as well as the breakdown of Care in the Community. However, the Edwards challenged the Report as being insufficient and their case against the Prison Service is still ongoing. The Report said:*

> *These features, taken together, amount to a systemic collapse of the protective mechanisms that ought to have operated to protect this vulnerable prisoner. These deficiencies resulted in the needless and tragic loss of a talented young man and much loved son and brother. (para. 46)*

In October 1998 the Bishop of Lincoln initiated a debate on the case of Christopher Edwards in the House of Lords. The Bishop of Ely also spoke and the Edwards family were in the gallery of the House of Lords to hear a Government Minister admit and express his regrets at what had happened. This debate showed that there was still a place for bishops in the House of Lords to bring issues of public policy into public debate. The Minister with responsibility for mental health matters, Paul Boateng, came to the House of Lords to listen to the debate. In the next two months the Government announced far-reaching changes for Care in the Community. It is hoped that these changes will mean that a death like Christopher's will not happen again in prison.

6

Vulnerability and the Sex Offender

Tim Newell

The context

There has been an increase in the rate of violent crime in the past 15 years and in the rate of the reporting of such crimes by victims. Similarly the fear of crime, particularly violent crime, has increased although there are recent signs of a decrease. The main area of concern for women is the fear of rape. The incidence of such crimes is much less than most people realize and yet the fear generated by one or two publicized offences can create considerable distress and can affect people's lifestyles as they seek to avoid risk. Even though the incidence is lower than expected there is good evidence that the actual number of rapes is four times higher than reported and that the experience of child molestation may be even higher. This must lead us to focus seriously on the nature of sex offences and those who commit them. An estimate that between 25 and 35 per cent of all adult women were sexually exploited by an adult male during their childhood or adolescence must suggest that the problem has reached epidemic proportions.

Our response

Our response within the criminal-justice process has been to increase the length of sentences for serious sex offenders, to establish closer supervision of known offenders when they are released from custody and to develop more effective interventions in the form of treatment programmes within prisons and in the community. However the full nature of our vulnerability to damaging inappropriate sexual behaviour remains uncertain and may be a cause for the extreme anger expressed when a known sex offender is at large. The dynamic of being relieved at having a scapegoat on whom to project all our own feelings, fantasies and even misbehaviour may explain the ease with which fear is generated and anger targeted in such instances. Within prison the same dynamic of separation of the sex offender from others is recognized as having many functions to fulfil as well as the personal safety of the individual. We are thus exploring a very complex and deeply emotional subject when considering vulnerability and sex offending.

Considerations

This chapter will look at the treatment of sex offenders in prisons as this episode in their life represents the most extreme expression of society's rejection of their behaviour and of them. The experience of imprisonment for all represents distinct kinds of risks, as it does for those who work within prisons. In particular the risk that prisoners face in relation to victimization by other prisoners must be addressed in discussing sex offenders. The treatment of sex offenders will be outlined as will the latest evidence of the risk of reconviction amongst such men. The concerns about the release into the community of serious sex offenders who remain dangerous will be considered and the arrangements for their supervision reviewed. Finally the latest plans for the containment of dangerous offenders whilst they remain a risk will be outlined.

Treatment for sex offenders

There has been considerable attention given to the treatment of sex offenders and although it is not possible to generalize about the factors associated with different types of sex offences, nevertheless it is possible to extract some characteristics which have been found to be present especially when considering treatment methods.

There is considerable evidence that childhood experiences of caregiver instability, institutional history, developmental history of abuse and some biological factors contribute towards adult features which could well lead to sexual assault. These features include fundamental aspects such as impaired relationships with adults, lack of empathy, degree and nature of anger, cognitive distortions, deviant sexual arousals and antisocial personality and lifestyle leading to impulsivity.

Treatments have been developed in various settings for the target areas identified above.

- Thus for 'impaired relationships with adults', treatment centres around social skills training, relaxation training, assertiveness training, self-esteem enhancement and systematic desensitization. The effectiveness of such methods remains questionable, despite the long tradition of their use.

- 'Lack of empathy' is addressed through victim empathy training, through childhood victim survivor's groups, and through the expressive therapies (art and drama). The evidence is that if victim empathy can be developed then there are effects on arousal, cognitive distortions and a more realistic self-esteem can emerge. There is much evidence that this aspect is present in offenders other than sexual ones and could be critical in many treatments.

- 'Degree and nature of anger' is helped through anger management, stress management training, through childhood victim survivor's group and through relapse prevention. Aggression to achieve victim compliance can vary considerably (instrumental anger) whilst expressive anger may be towards any available target. It has to be recognized that anger plays a part in sexual offences and that methods of managing aggression which work for the individual need to be developed with the offender.

- 'Cognitive distortions' or irrational ideas, thoughts and attitudes which serve to perpetuate denial, foster minimization of impact on victims and justify further sexually aggressive behaviour. These matters can be addressed through cognitive restructuring, not just by focusing on the attitudes of the offender but also to consider the effects on the victim and thereby create discomfort for the offender. It is also by this method that victim empathy can be developed as well. Thus a group which focuses on childhood victim survival will also help restructure distortions.

• 'Sexual fantasy and deviant sexual arousal' are addressed through covert sensitization, olfactory aversion, masturbatory satiation and pharmacotherapy. These treatments focus on either decreasing sexual arousal through behavioural means such as aversion therapy or on increasing appropriate arousal involving exposure to appropriate sexual material. Organic treatment has become increasingly popular as a complement to psychological treatment, using antiandrogens to reduce sexual drive by reducing levels of testosterone or antidepressants to enhance serotonin transmission which is considered to inhibit sexual arousal.

• 'Antisocial personality, lifestyle impulsivity' have been central to much discussion about criminality lately. Treatment which has been tried but has not been considered very successful includes self-control and impulse management, stress management, relapse prevention and pharmacotherapy.

The vulnerability of the community

Given the failure of more traditional remedies for offending such as deterrence and incapacitation for reducing sexual violence, other interventions must be actively sought. There is however a resistance to treating sex offenders because it is perceived as a 'humane' response to behaviour we find despicable. However if the overriding goal is to reduce the number of victims, as well as the cost incurred by victimization and if rehabilitation can be shown to reduce the likelihood of reoffence then it is imperative that we overcome our resistance to treating such offenders and work towards minimization of the risk for others. There is increasing evidence that if treatment programmes are established to evidence-based effective criteria standards then there can indeed be a reduction in recidivism. The vulnerability of the public can be reduced through formal treatment courses, either held within custody or in the community.

Treatment inside

Within the Prison Service treatment programmes for sex offenders address different factors which are directly targeted at the offending (offence-specific); there are also other treatments for interpersonal and emotional functioning (personality deficits).

Offence-specific approaches include:

- **reducing minimization** – the offender should acknowledge the scope and seriousness of his offending and take responsibility for it;

- **enhancing victim empathy** – the offender should be vividly aware of the scope and seriousness of the damage / distress caused to his victims;

- **relapse prevention** – the offender should be aware of the factors which put him at risk of reoffending and should have developed strategies for controlling these factors.

As well as these very specifically focused areas of work there are more general levels of behaviours which are directly relevant to sexual offending but which do not need to be addressed through the examination of the individual's own offences. This would include, for example, the belief in sexual entitlement ('I am entitled to gratify my needs'), belief in rape myths or similar general beliefs about classes of victims, also certain kinds of sexual interest (say, in children), or some cognitive deficits (for example, difficulty distinguishing the kinds of sexual approach women will find abusive). These areas can be considered as **offence-related** factors.

At a still more general level, there are **personality deficits** which are aspects of interpersonal or emotional functioning which may contribute to sexual offending but which involve no content which is particular to it.

Examples would be general psychopathic traits, problems being emotionally intimate with adults, deficits in assertiveness skill etc.

The Sex Offender Treatment Programme (SOTP) which has been working in our prisons for the past eight years addresses offending behaviour through a well-structured and delivered course based on the disciplines which have been demonstrated to work in reducing offending. Offence specific factors are directly targeted by the SOTP but it is unlikely that the follow-through of the offence-related areas would be addressed unless the environment was particularly supportive to the treatment programme. It is only in therapeutic community settings, however, that the personality deficits are addressed in any systematic and sustained manner, enabling offenders to explore their behaviour over time in a setting of a supportive yet challenging community. There is also good evidence that offence-related issues arising from distorted attitudes can be most relevantly addressed within the therapeutic community setting.

The treatment of sex offenders can lead to a reduction in the risk to the public of reoffending and the range of treatments being developed, along with a closer assessment process, will enable greater certainty to be gained in this subject.

The vulnerability of the offender

The risk to some prisoners of victimization by others leads to major structural adjustments to the management of the prison population at national and local level. All prisoners share certain vulnerabilities and in the appendix to this chapter there is a sensitive description of one man's experience of this. There have been very few examinations of the risk that prisoners face whilst in custody, although those which have been carried out show that the recording of events within official statistics cannot be trusted. Figures for assaults, drugs, AIDS and self-injury are much under-recorded. It is an open secret amongst prisoners and staff that the prison is deeply given to conspiracies of silence, exercises of discretion, negotiation and haphazard record-keeping. This clearly means that the fact that prisoners are at risk of harm is a commonplace which is casually acknowledged.

Risk in prisons

Risk is a multi-dimensional concept. The combination of risks to prisoners, including the victimization or exploitation by other prisoners, or of arbitrary or oppressive treatment by prison authorities, and a diminished sense of personal power, are conditions likely to produce a sense of dread in most prisoners. It is clear however that neither risk nor fear is evenly distributed either between prisons or between individuals and groups of prisoners. The sex offender is in the group which attracts the most attention of prisoners and staff and so makes them particularly vulnerable, so much so that separate areas of prisons are set up to segregate those who have sought protection from other prisoners.

The concept of risk should not purely be reduced to that of victimization by other prisoners because of the nature of their offence. All prisoners are vulnerable to other factors such as the health risks in prisons, to suicide and self-harm, to arbitrary, oppressive or discriminatory treatment, to their post-release prospects in employment and family life, and to their chances of returning to prison.

Risk assessment and risk reduction are central to prison managers' and staff's concepts of what they are doing daily and indeed is often the way that decisions are justified. Staff are very sensitive to some risks but not at all to others. Governors are particularly sensitive to the threat of riot and serious escape and such 'high consequence risks' can dominate approaches to prison management at the expense of more mundane harms. Because of the anxiety about 'high consequence risks' there is a strong wish to conserve order and routine and thus an aversion to change. Prison managers have to make difficult judgements about individual and collective goods using utilitarian criteria and uncertain information.

Within the key decisions made, the main ones concern those who are considered particularly dangerous or troublesome and about those who are considered to be particularly at risk. Special measures have to be taken for both groups and are justified on the grounds of reducing the likelihood of risk.

In our prisons the most acute decision made about these groups is that of segregation under Rule 45 of the Prison Rules, which can result in the special units for disruptive prisoners called Close Supervision Centres (CSC) and the Vulnerable Prisoner Units (VPUs) for those who are at risk from other prisoners because of their offence or their behaviour in custody. These decisions are high in risk, they are designed to prevent future harms and so are about the consequences if no action were taken. They are often based on limited information – rumour, 'intelligence' received, induction, impression, reputation. They are highly discretionary, and hence open to abuse and ulterior motivations. They are emergency powers and are subject therefore to careful scrutiny after the event by the independent group appointed by the Home Secretary, the Board of Visitors.

For the prisoner in need of protection there are several vulnerabilities or risks:

- The risk of victimization on 'normal location', and the experience of living in fear;

- The risk of tedium, isolation, deprivation and possible discrimination whilst living 'on the rule';

- The risk that the measures taken for the prisoner's protection are inadequate, whilst identifying him to his victimizers;

- The risk of being unable to come off 'the rule' if a prisoner so wishes.

The permanent existence of a vulnerable population poses difficult problems. It is sometimes cynically thought that the persecution of sex offenders and others has latent benefits for the authorities. It can arise from stable hierarchies of power amongst prisoners, it can permit a face-saving normalization for other offenders and it allows ideological affinity to be demonstrated between prisoners and staff. There has been much discussion about how the number of prisoners on Rule 45 could be reduced, looking at the regimes of certain prisons such as Grendon and Littlehey and looking at the culture in other countries where there is no such segregation. However it is unlikely that those who feel vulnerable because of their offence will risk the prospect of integration.

Prisons are continually struggling to secure routine in the face of chronic conflict and problems of legitimacy. If a prison can produce a sufficient level of trust, minimize critical situations and gain a sufficient degree of legitimacy in the eyes of its captive population, then that might represent some form of sustainable order.

Prison risks

It is possible to consider the range of vulnerabilities faced by all prisoners and particularly by sex offenders and then propose a model under which the development of the work with offenders could be developed.

There are risks to life and health from:

- victimization;

- disease, especially HIV and Hepatitis B;

- exacerbated risk of suicide and self-harm.

There are risks of oppressive/arbitrary treatment and legal vulnerability from:

- decisions made through the courts and the right of appeal;

- decisions made locally within a prison by staff who exercise discretion at all levels.

There are also risks to 'social being' through:

- employment, earning capacity being reduced;

- family relations, social ties, housing;

- probability of returning to prison.

All these vulnerabilities make the prison experience one of great risk for offenders and particularly sex offenders.

On release

The process of release for sex offenders has become increasingly risky particularly if their offence is well known and if there is evidence that they have done little to reduce the risk they represent. On their release sex offenders are subject to periods of supervision under current legislation and the probation services have developed skills in managing such people over time with police support when necessary. The risk and the vulnerability continues as we are aware from recent high-profile cases when vigilante crowds have demanded the moving on of particular released prisoners, when men have had to be kept in semi-secure conditions for their own protection even when they are technically free.

The ultimate risk assessment

With the current concern about the treatment of offenders with serious personality disorders following the Ashworth Inquiry and the review of the arrangements under the Mental Health Act, there is increasing anxiety that serious offenders could be released into the community whilst still posing a considerable risk. The call for a 'reviewable' sentence for those assessed as having a severe personality disorder may well include those who have committed the most serious sex offences. The sentence would depend upon an assessment about the personality of the offender rather than upon the nature or gravity of the offence. Following this assessment, a reviewable sentence would be passed which would entail a tariff for the punitive element as with life sentences at present, but then a process of risk assessment based on the likelihood of reoffending would be carried out so that only those considered safe for release would be discharged from custody. The custodial experience would not necessarily be in a prison setting as there are plans to establish an entirely new form of custodial agency between the Special Hospitals and the Prison Service. This process should ensure that the public are better protected from a high risk group of offenders who currently can be released with few sanctions over them. The cost of this safety may well be considered too high in terms of the denting of human rights through the sentence being based not so much on what a prisoner has done but rather upon the sort of person he is. Alternative procedures are being actively worked upon which are a greater respecter of the rights of the individual, but which are challenging to those who have not considered the possibility of change in the criminal-justice process.

A model for the future

There are elements within best practice in the criminal-justice process and within the tradition of 'what works' of a model for the treatment of sex offenders within our culture which would reduce the risks and vulnerabilities for us all, including the offender. The model will not be developed without much commitment from communities as well as from the leadership of the authorities who are concerned with decision-making about criminal-justice matters.

Restorative justice has been developed as a concept for the past twenty years or so and there is now evidence that the ideas and values which it represents may well be sufficiently attractive for it to be developed on a national scale. The ideas are simple but the practice and the application can be complicated and sensitive.

At the centre is the idea that when a crime is committed the act is not against the state but against the victim. As a consequence the main effort of the process of justice should be on putting right the wrong brought about by the crime. The person who committed the offence is responsible for that process and the community is interested in ensuring that the balance or stability of life before the offence is restored.

Thus there are three main elements in working out this model: the **victim**, the **offender** and the **community**. All three are involved in the process of justice and there are procedures within the decision-making about offences which can take the three areas into consideration and act in restorative rather than retributive ways. Rather than focusing on the offender and seeking to punish them, the emphasis of restorative justice is upon the victim and seeks ways to ensure that the harm brought about by the offence can be reduced. For sex offenders this is a difficult concept to work at but it is a challenge to those who are seriously committed to the values of respect for the individual, the acceptance of responsibility for behaviour leading to better involvement and citizenship, and the need to take the harm to victims seriously enough to ensure understanding and explanation. The belief in the sanctity of the individual leads us to consider restorative justice as a way to bring beliefs into action in addressing sex offenders, in helping their victims and in enabling communities to support each other despite the fear which follows the risk.

In a restorative model the emphasis following a sex offence would be upon ensuring that the safety of the victim was paramount to any consideration for future action. Any action in relation to the offender would be dependent upon their acceptance of their responsibility for the offence. If they did not admit the offence and yet there remained good evidence against them then the normal judicial process would continue. If they did admit it, however, it may then be possible at some stage of the proceedings, before, during or after the court hearing, that there would be some dialogue between the victim and the offender with their supporting family members to discuss and review the events which took place. This can only happen if all parties agree to the process. Through this dialogue, which can happen within each other's presence or at a distance, the victim can have their questions and anxieties answered and the emphasis upon the future stability of the victim be the important focus. Despite the sensitivities of the sexual nature of offences there is the same need for anxieties to be addressed and for us to be able to develop a procedure and language to express the consequences and for the taking of responsibility to be informed rather than neutral.

The aim as far as the offenders are concerned is to accept responsibility for their behaviour, to understand the effect of their behaviour upon their victims and to address their behaviour through the variety of treatments described above so that they do not commit further offences and create further victims.

It is in working towards this model of restorative justice for sex offenders that those with a belief in the power of forgiveness will be most tested. Can we accept back into full community (communion) those who have committed the most frightening of offences, once they have shown they have accepted responsibility for their offence (confession) and have undergone treatment in custody or in the community (reparation) so that they can return to take up their role in society as full members (atonement)? The task for those with faith is demanding and challenges us to put our beliefs into action with those who are the 'most despised and rejected'.

Appendix to Chapter 6

What I Think about Vulnerability

John Wrigglesworth

Vulnerability is something we all share. It will differ in its specific manifestation for us as individuals but we will all know what it feels like to be vulnerable.

First of all we have to accept that at some stage in our lives we are going to feel vulnerable. That is not always as simple as it sounds because we do not have a clear-cut definition of what being vulnerable means for the individual. The dictionary simply states that it means to be open to hurt. We are often hurt without feeling vulnerable. We are so adept at masking our fears that it is not easy to accept them for what they are, especially at the time when emotions are running rampant. When my partner was late I would get really angry and fight with her but not simply because she was late, rather it had more to do with my own fears. I thought she might have been hurt or that she had fallen out with me, but I never told her that at the time. I felt comfortable with the anger and uncomfortable with the feelings of vulnerability.

I also believe vulnerability is linked with how we feel about ourselves. My self-image is very poor and as a result of that I can be hurt by things most people would laugh at. However I have learned how to deal with it to some extent. I thought at one time that nobody else was vulnerable. I would watch them doing things with ease that made me tremble at the mere thought. Take the school disco. I had to go but no way was I going to dance and yet my peers found it so easy – or so it seemed to me. Wild stallions would not get me on the floor, although the Osmonds' *Crazy Horses* nearly did, which is very sad and shows my age. Now I know that everyone suffers from fears, but they do not let them stop them from doing things, and that is the difference. I did let my fears, my vulnerability stop me from doing things I wanted to do and was good at. I became isolated as a result, which led to even greater problems.

Another aspect of how I feel about myself involves the way I am feeling at the time. If I am high in spirits then my partner being late might not faze me as much as it would if I was feeling down. This can contradict the base self-image I have of myself but in reality it is only that the feelings I have at the time override the deeper truth, yet I would argue they are the more powerful because they are constant. They will surface in the future after boiling away inside me for minutes, hours, days or weeks. I am more aware of them now and try to resolve issues as they arrive and not use old arguments to win new battles.

I still believe vulnerability is at the heart of my problems. I've spent so long dealing with my core problems that I convinced myself that I had resolved my feelings of vulnerability. The truth is that I have – but only to the same extent that most people have. I try not to let my vulnerability stop me from walking out onto the dance floor these days, but it is difficult. I can give the appearance of being assertive and in control but inside I feel like a kitten and this was brought home to me recently. I am moving to another prison this week. It's a good progressive move but there is a cost to pay. I will be leaving people who are more important to me than I had previously admitted to myself. I will be leaving a place where I have been safe to explore my innermost psyche and address issues that caused so much pain to others and myself and try to resolve them. I looked at my vulnerability and thought that was it. It was resolved. The sad truth is that I will always be vulnerable and that is hard to admit because I don't like the idea that I will always be open to hurt. However, it also means that I am aware now how it feels to be vulnerable and because I don't like it I try not to make others feel like that through my actions.

Welcome to the real world, I almost hear you shout, but living with it has become my constant problem. The guilt I feel for my past means that I judge myself harshly. That means, in effect, that I am open to hurt and see it even when it wasn't meant. My perception is marred by the way I feel about myself. My view can twist the most innocent of gestures into confirmation that I deserved to be slighted because I am a bad person.

How we choose to deal with the problem is important. I have learned to accept it as a given fact, and, rather than worry about it, I try to deal with it in the best way that I can. Other people deal with it in different ways, some more destructive than others. In prison, people tend to stick to a strata system that has the 'gangster' at the top and the child molester at the bottom. In a way, I see that as a way of dealing with prison and the vulnerability that entails. When you have your liberty taken from you then by extension you become vulnerable. You have no power, and by your actions have put yourself in an underclass. The staff in their prison uniforms and their chains and keys control your life. If you find someone that you can look down on then you are a little less vulnerable. I think it is the same in all walks of life and another way of avoiding that feeling of vulnerability.

Relationships of every kind entail feelings of vulnerability. A part of my isolation was to avoid those pitfalls because they had caused me no end of grief. However, that was no use because it meant I missed out on the benefits that having a relationship brings too. Now that I have friends that are important to me then I have a responsibility to live up to their expectations, and vice versa of course. I still feel vulnerable but I trust them enough to be comfortable with my feelings and that they share them in their own way too.

Vulnerability then is not a feeling anyone would enjoy, but nor is it a completely negative experience either. How we learn to deal with it within ourselves and how we learn to help others in their hour of need is more important. Too many people try to avoid it in ways that cause more grief to themselves than accepting it in the first place. Or they transfer other feelings in its place and use them to strike out and make others feel bad in a vague attempt to make themselves feel better. If we learn to accept our own vulnerability, then we might learn how to stop others feeling vulnerable because of our actions. We do not like the feeling, so why make others feel that way?

7

Prisoners' Families

The Forgotten Victims

Lucy Gampell and Janet Harber

Someone's kicked the bottom out of your world and you are
falling through this black tunnel and you've got nothing to put
your feet on. It's a harrowing experience, the emotions you
go through, it was like a kaleidoscope.

(A prisoner's wife)

In 1998 approximately 127,000 people were committed to custody by
the courts, resulting in an all-time high prison population for England
and Wales. The figures show few signs of abating. As a result, an ever-
increasing number of families find themselves with the experience of
having a family member in prison, and many of them are in touch with the
criminal-justice system for the first time.

The criminal-justice process and prisoners' families

It is not possible to fully understand the total vulnerability experienced by
the families of people in prison just by looking at the Prison System alone.
The Prison System forms one part of a criminal-justice process in which
the families of someone accused of a crime find themselves marginalized,
ignored and treated as 'guilty by association'. Indeed, they become seen
as *prisoners'* families, rather than as individual members of a family who,

through no fault of their own, find themselves intrinsically linked to someone in prison. This position of association renders them vulnerable to a system, that, whilst it is there to protect the public, differentiates between the general public, legitimate victims and the offenders' families – the forgotten victims. The lack of public understanding and largely unsympathetic media coverage place additional strain on families, some of whom even find themselves hounded from their homes or having to move their children to different schools to avoid victimization or harassment.

Prisoners' children are at particular risk. Over 140,000 children per year are estimated to have a parent in prison and the impact of the experience on them can have longlasting effect. For a child, the arrest of a parent or sibling means a central figure in their lives has suddenly (and often inexplicably) been taken away from them. Many arrests take place in the home in the middle of the night when the police know a suspect is most likely to be there and off-guard. However, imagine the experience from the perspective of a child whose home is abruptly, noisily and sometimes aggressively entered by the police, who then take away one of their parents: 'When the police came, I thought I was never going to see her again'. (*A prisoner's child*)

An experience such as this can then lead to possible antipathy towards other figures of authority such as teachers and prison officers. Furthermore, the arrest marks the beginning of a complicated and often lengthy experience, characterized by uncertainty – something with which children in particular find it hard to cope. Negative media coverage, demonizing the offender as an 'evil monster', hounding by the Press and the reactions of people around them are particularly distressing to children. All of this can have a detrimental effect on them, including threatening their educational performance and future life-chances. Many children experience bullying, teasing or are worried about the teacher's own prejudices but do want to be able to talk with teachers or an appropriate person about what is going on.

For parents, what and when to tell the children is one of the hardest issues they have to face. Many find the task too daunting and choose to make up stories instead. They need advice and support to help them and their children through the experience, but most never receive specialist help. The uncertainty and distress caused by the criminal-justice process adds to people's feelings of vulnerability. At court, the defendant's relatives receive none of the support or protection given to the victims of crime and they can find themselves in the public gallery alongside the victim's family or prey to the frequently unscrupulous behaviour of the media, hungry for the latest salacious crime story. Some families even have to go into hiding to escape the Press. They also find themselves listening to accounts of people they love which are beyond their recognition:

> We didn't recognise in any of the things that we heard or saw the son or brother that we knew. We know that he wasn't perfect, but we recognized nothing in him of what we were being asked to accept.
>
> *(A family member)*

Once the accused is remanded or sentenced to custody, the family has no right to see them in the court, and are left to fend for themselves, both practically and emotionally. Many families find their lives dominated by what is happening around them as they then try to face the consequences, such as stigma, shame, isolation, financial hardship, guilt and stress. The very reasons for their needing help and support often prevent them from asking for it because of these feelings of shame and stigma. At present there are less than 25 organizations offering specialist support to prisoners' families and many of these are small voluntary groups usually set up by someone who has themselves been through the experience. Each year a number of people try to start up a new group. However, due to the complexities of getting it established and the recognition of the enormity of the task ahead, many do not come to fruition.

Parents of prisoners, in particular, try to find answers by looking at themselves, thinking they must be to blame 'I thought to myself, well I have fallen by the wayside here, am I to blame for this, is my wife to blame for this?' *(A prisoner's father)*

Families' problems are compounded by the lack of basic information given to them at any stage of the process, leaving them frequently in the dark as to what is happening and unaware of the availability of help and support. Yet, maintaining good prisoner family and community ties is one of the most significant factors that affects the likelihood of further offending after release. The Woolf Report into the serious prison riots of 1990 concluded that:

> If the destructive effects of imprisonment are to be reduced so that the prospects of the prisoner not reoffending can be improved, it is critical that, where possible, the prisoner's links with his family and the community should be maintained.

A Home Office review of all the literature relating to recidivism and family ties[1] pointed to studies in the UK and the USA which clearly supported the findings of Burnett and others[2] who concluded:

> . . . the quality of an offender's relationships with his partner and the degree of influence which partners can bring to bear can be pivotal in decisions to desist.

Despite this, little is done to support, sustain or strengthen family relationships whilst the offender is in prison. We live in a society which considers itself to be one that cares for its less fortunate members – a core principle of any religious doctrine – yet it would seem that for many, prisoners' families are undeserving of sympathy and support. Does the paucity of support available present a challenge to church congregations to address the needs of those with a family member in prison? What answer is available to the question 'Is the church the first or last place to which a family in trouble will turn?'

The Prison System

We turn now to the Prison System itself and the interface between prisons and the visitors to them, on whom the prisons so readily depend.

The day-to-day work of the Prison Service is governed by a series of Standing Orders which relate to their operations. Standing Order Five states:

> It is one of the roles of the Prison Service to ensure that the socially harmful effects of an inmate's removal from normal life are so far as possible minimised and that his contacts with the outside world are maintained. Outside contacts are therefore encouraged between an inmate and his family and friends.

The importance of visits to prisoners is widely acknowledged and was reinforced both in the 1991 National Prisons Survey and the Woolf Report. The Woolf Report went further by linking the importance placed by prisoners on contact with their families to the safety and stability of the prison. The Report concluded that:

> It is highly desirable for the stable running of a prison and for the prospects of the prisoner leading a law abiding life after release that, whenever practicable, he should be accommodated as near to his home and community as possible. The problem of holding prisoners remote from their homes and visitors was a very evident factor during the disturbance. So was the number of prisoners transferred from other prisons which were nearer their homes.

Lord Woolf also argued strongly for the need for a balance between custody, care and justice, if the Prison System were to achieve its goals in protecting the public, preparing people for release and treating those in their care (and the people visiting them) with humanity. The Prison Service initially accepted much of the spirit and content of the Woolf Report and shortly afterwards created the Family Ties Unit at Prison Service Headquarters. This Unit convened a working group, known as the Family Ties Consultative Group and invited a range of voluntary organizations to be part of the forum which would meet quarterly to raise issues around prisoners' ties with their families. Members include the Federation of Prisoners' Families Support Groups, the Prison Reform

Trust, NACRO, the Howard League, children's organizations and practitioners working with prisoners' families. However, as with so many aspects of prison policy, family contact is affected by political considerations and external influences on the Prison Service. Families find themselves caught up in situations outside their control or understanding but which have potentially enormous consequences for them. These include changes in emphasis and policy led by Government dicta (such as the mid-1990s emphasis on security, the introduction of the Incentives and Earned Privileges Scheme and the reduction in Home Leave), the extent of discretion afforded to Governors resulting in a huge variation in the application of procedures and practice between different establishments and policy created centrally which takes little account of the impact it will have on visitors (although opportunities for consultation with the Prison Service are currently improving as recognition of the need to consider the effects on families grows).

As has already been said, there is very limited information made readily available to families directing them to appropriate services, support or financial assistance, and many face the period of a loved one's imprisonment unaware of even the most basic information that is available to them. Their vulnerability is aggravated by their love for the person in prison and their feelings of loyalty to the prisoner. Many feel under an obligation to visit, yet are given little, if any, information to help them prepare for the stressful experience of visiting. For example, many families have costly, arduous journeys to the prison, which could involve several changes in transport often with young children in tow. Those on a low income and in receipt of benefit should be eligible for statutory support under the Assisted Prison Visits Scheme, yet time and again, families are not told about its existence for months, or even years after they start visiting. On arrival at the prison they may have to wait some considerable time before going in, yet many prisons still do not have a visitors' centre or waiting area. The visits process itself is frequently stressful and many families find the searching procedures and attitudes towards them demeaning. The visit is also unnatural with neither party wanting to worry the other one by saying what is really on their mind. 'We would talk about how we were both keeping. But I don't tell him everything. I don't want him worrying.' (*A prisoner's wife*)

For children, the visit is once again a stark reminder of how imprisonment punishes the family too. It is essential that prisons look more at meeting the needs of children visiting by providing suitably staffed and equipped play areas, holding family days and ensuring some mechanism which allows a meaningful relationship to develop between a parent in prison and their child. Meeting the needs of children on visits also benefits the parents who need time alone on visits, as well as people visiting without children who do not want to be constantly disrupted by the presence of bored or unsettled children.

Despite the fact that the Prison Service readily acknowledges the importance of visits both to the prisoner's morale and prison stability, there still appears to be an inherent prison culture which sees prisoners' families as at best a resource, and at worst a threat to security and a nuisance. The treatment families receive by officers and gate staff can make or break a visit. Prison policy often increases the family's emotional vulnerability to the demands of the prisoner. The Incentives and Earned Privileges Scheme was formulated on the premise that families would obligingly meet the 'rewards' on offer. Yet for families, the pressure of making an extra visit, providing clothes, possessions or private cash, might be more than they can manage, yet they do not want to let the prisoner down. Conversely, a prisoner's level on the scheme can change rapidly altering his visits entitlement, but the first the family might know of this is on turning up for a visit of one to two hours to be told it will only last for half an hour. This might seem reasonable from the prison's point of view, but the family may well have spent several hours getting to the prison expecting a longer visit. The same issue applies when a prisoner has been put on a closed visit. Security measures and anti-drugs strategies, whilst ultimately in everyone's best interest, frequently disregard the position of families. A prisoner who fails a mandatory drugs test will generally be put on closed visits, but again it is rare for the prison to tell the person visiting. This kind of information is vitally important to families, especially if they are planning to bring children with them on the visit; many families choose not to visit at all under closed conditions, rather than having to subject their children to this form of visit. Whilst it would be wrong to suggest that no families are responsible for bringing drugs into prison on visits, they may be doing so as a result of extreme psychological and emotional pressures being put on them by the prison. Their bonds of affection and fears over what might happen to the prisoner or even their children if they do not comply with the request result in some becoming soft targets in the problem of drugs in prison.

The way forward

There is no question of an ordinary prison visit providing a real opportunity for quality contact; however, the more visitors are prepared for the visit, the greater the chance of that visit being a positive experience. The Prison Service will shortly be publishing a general first-stop information leaflet giving guidance to visitors to prison. This has been produced jointly with the Federation of Prisoners' Families Support Groups and the Prison Reform Trust. However, as ever, it is primarily left to the voluntary sector to ensure such material is both written and made available to families. For example, information on preparing children for visits has been produced by the Ormiston Children & Families Trust.[3] A group of voluntary sector organizations, including the Federation, has also been involved in producing a *Visitors' Charter* which is currently being piloted in the Yorkshire and Central Prison Service areas. This calls for the following minimum standards of treatment:

- Clear, up-to-date information should be made available to all visitors to prisons prior to their first visits and whenever procedures or circumstances change;

- All prison staff who come into contact with visitors should receive training on the issues facing prisoners' families and on general customer relations;

- The needs of children visiting prison should be recognized and appropriate provision made;

- Visitors should be consulted about visits provisions and facilities;

- A complaints procedure should be drawn up and made readily available to visitors;

- Visits should be organized in such a way as to allow the best possible contact between the prisoner and visitors.

The Prison Service will shortly be embarking on a comprehensive review of visits which will involve the Federation. It is our hope that this might result in many of the practical difficulties families face on visits being overcome. One initiative favoured by many of those working with families (and the Chief Inspector of Prisons) is the system adopted in Scotland of Family Contact Development Officers. A couple of Young Offenders Institutions are currently piloting similar models, but we believe families should have access to a dedicated person at every prison who can help with their queries or concerns.

In the absence of any such post being created at all prisons, it is worth considering, at least in the short term, whether there is a role here for the Prison Chaplaincy and what issues this would raise both for chaplains and families. For chaplains their existing responsibilities already more than fill the time available. Could trained chaplain's assistants and volunteers enable assistance to be provided? How would this impact on families seeking information and support from a prison? Families of other faiths, those with no religious affiliations and those with an antipathy to any church-based provider of services may be extremely reluctant to seek help via this route. The Prison Chaplaincy may have been the obvious place to locate responsibilities for prisoners' families in the earlier part of the twentieth century when chaplains had the primary role for welfare within prisons. Today family needs relate more widely and impinge upon a number of areas of prison procedures, requiring a broader remit best served by a dedicated person.

Our model of justice regards offences as being committed against the state and so leaves victims outside its processes and the families of offenders unrecognized. So what would be required to ensure that the needs of the families of prisoners were automatically included in the responsibilities of the Prison Service and other criminal justice agencies? The concept of Restorative Justice sees crime as a fundamental violation of people and interpersonal relationships. It recognizes that victims and the community are harmed by crime and need restoration. The family of an offender may be a primary or secondary victim; witnesses are also directly affected. Restorative Justice attempts, as far as possible, to put right the wrongs, to restore relationships, to mend and to heal the damage caused by the offender. The concept engenders hope for the future. Within such a model the families of prisoners would be recognized as an indispensable part of the process. Their vulnerability would be reduced by the acceptance of them as important to the prisoner, as suffering because of the offender's actions and as being part of the community.

Furthermore, families need to be viewed as a positive resource in the fight against crime by the Prison Service and the wider community. They should be given the opportunity to be involved throughout the prisoner's sentence in the induction programme and sentence planning and preparation for release courses. It is only by seeing families in this way that their own vulnerability will be minimized and the prisoner be given an improved chance of leading a law-abiding life on release. Until then, families will continue to live in the shadows of the offender's action, marginalized by a system that depends on them, ostracized by the community around them and vulnerable to the many pressures and demands put upon them.

III

The Christian Response

8

Prison Chaplaincy

Robert Hardy and David Fleming

Plate 4: Prison Chaplains represent 'the Church' and 'God' to the prison community. *HM Prison Service Chaplaincy.*

An offender can be punished . . . But to punish and not to restore, that is the greatest of all offences. If a man takes unto himself God's right to punish, then he must also take upon himself God's promise to restore.[1]

In his Annual Report for 1997–8, Her Majesty's Chief Inspector of Prisons writes:

No praise can be too high for the work of the Chaplaincy in the prisons, by which I mean the multi-faith ministry that is delivered by teams of Chaplains of all denominations. Because their work encompasses prisoners, staff and their families, their influence is felt in every part of a prison . . . A strong Chaplaincy team is an undoubted influence for good in a prison and in these days of overcrowding and resource shortages, nothing positive should be undermined.

The Chief Inspector's words are an indication of the value he places upon the ministry of Prison Chaplains, but also clear evidence that that ministry is not simply the work of the Church of England alone. That said, the Church of England has a long and honourable history of work in prison. The Act of 1773, John Howard's famous journal of investigation *The State of Prisons in England and Wales,* and Robert Peel's Gaol Act of 1823 were milestones marking the formal participation of a Chaplain in the life of the prison.

In 1816 the National Penitentiary opened at Millbank, heralding a period when a variety of methods were used to prove religion was the answer to crime. It soon became clear, however, that even the coercion of the penitentiary cannot bring about change without a heart which is open to the love of God. Equally, it became clear that improvements in the Prison System, where prisoners were no longer herded together in enforced cohabitation, should be maintained and improved. The ministry of the Chaplain continued to be enshrined in the various Prison Acts up to, and including, that of the most recent in 1952. That Act gives significant emphasis that the 'Chaplain' should be a priest of the Church of England, properly licensed by the Bishop. It also makes it clear that visiting ministers should be appointed for other faiths and denominations. At the last census of the religion of prisoners, there were over 40 different faiths and denominations.

The Prison Act places the Chaplaincy firmly within the context of the prison, but it also underlines the ambivalence of a Chaplain's ministry. A Chaplain has a dual accountability; accountable as a servant of the Church, but also as an employee of the state. This lays upon a Chaplain an obligation not only to work within the system, but also and always to examine that system and, where necessary, to challenge and to work to change it. The Chaplain has to walk the tightrope of working within the system and yet being seen as independent of it: to balance the ability to feed both ideas and criticisms into the management structures, without being too closely locked in and identified with them. The physical requirement to carry keys identifies the Chaplain with the system, a compromise which has to be accepted in spite of the misunderstandings it might create. Keys, however, also open doors. They enable 'Statutory Duties' to become pastoral events. The Statutory Duties laid down in the Prison Rules and Standing Orders ensure that prisoners are seen by a Chaplain as they come into prison, and daily if they are in the Segregation Unit or the Health Centre. No member of the Chaplaincy team is limited by that which is defined as 'statutory', and those duties often become the springboard to involvement in the whole life of the prison, in different ways and at different levels with prisoners and staff and their families.

No one can enter a prison without becoming aware that this is one of the extreme environments of life. Here are people deprived of many of those features which make life tolerable – freedom of movement and choice and restrictions on normal social and sexual intercourse. Prisons are places of constant movement and noise. They are authoritarian and regimented. They bring together the violent, the immature and the weak-willed. As institutions, they cannot avoid creating anxiety and loneliness. Not infrequently, they give opportunity to the bully and the pretentious. All this makes any ministry in prison a sobering and testing experience. It is front-line work of care and calls from those who undertake it a considerable degree of self-knowledge and a sure grasp of faith and personal value and belief.

Arrest and reception in prison are traumatic and dehumanizing experiences. Most people in prison need help in coping with the loss of self-respect. In one sense, they lose their identity. They become a number. Their physical conditions are basic and limited. Their companionship is enforced, and their life is almost totally restricted and controlled. Anyone therefore who accords them dignity and worth – in Christian terms those who remind them that they are still children beloved of God – begins to set them on the road to redemption and hope. Most often these qualities are communicated informally, and sometimes the most effective pastoral care offered in prison is in casual conversation and informal contact. In doing this one frequently finds there is a refreshing spontaneity and a direct honesty amongst prison inmates, and anyone who ministers to them needs a ready sense of humour and an ability to be alert and sensitive to the opportunities for pastoral contact which the Prison System provides.

At the same time there is a need to balance both a judgemental and an accepting attitude in the face of encounters where often there are strong feelings of anger, guilt and sin. Indulgence is rarely helpful here. To emphasize the personal is right, but to concentrate on the individual is wrong, and frequently the Chaplain has to make a delicate judgement in response. Sometimes a firmer attitude can give the offender some real framework for support. On other occasions an accepting attitude is more advantageous; it encourages confidence and self-awareness. Whatever course is adopted, the aim should always be to help the offender accept his situation and understand it in such a way that he himself is brought to pass judgement upon it. Only this new insight can bring real hope, and the possibility of establishing a new beginning. Here, again, a firm grasp of theological insight and possibility is an important advantage. One needs to know what one believes, and be able to communicate it in simple, direct terms.

Almost all offenders respond to a good listener. Most of them can tell a good tale, and whereas not all answers are necessarily truthful, there is often a real willingness amongst prisoners themselves to deal with direct and personal questions. Sensitivity on the part of the listener is clearly important, but being alongside the offender in a total sense is equally significant. It is not for nothing that in the scriptures truth and freedom are connected. Nor is it by accident that the prophet Ezekiel could describe his ministry of pastoral care towards the prisoners of Babylon in terms of listening and being alongside. 'I sat where they sat' can still provide a touchstone for ministry in prison today.

Very few prisons have more than one chapel. Whenever a new prison chapel is dedicated or an old one refurbished, it is always as an ecumenical chapel: a witness to Christ and Christian Unity at the heart of the prison community. Attendance at worship is always on a voluntary basis, but proportionately it is often very high in relation to the church attendance of the general population. Of course, it is possible to be cynical about this, but there is no doubt that the worship of a prison creates a real opportunity for giving inmates new vision and hope, implanting the message of the gospel, and adding immeasurably to the quality of life. Most Chaplains would testify warmly to the enrichment of prison worship through the presence of Christians from 'outside'.

It should be obvious from all this that there are enormous opportunities for people of faith to work in prisons. The community of care needs to be imparted not by individual Chaplains, volunteers or other staff, but by the community of faith if truly the Good News is to become incarnate. Prison Chaplains represent their faith community, they represent the 'Church' and 'God'. Clearly, they are mandated by their respective denomination but the way in which they work across denominational boundaries is also critical. Chaplains need to express what deeply unites them instead of stressing their denominational differences. As Henri Nouwen has expressed it:

> The witness for Christ is a common witness in which those who want to be of service begin by serving each other, washing each other's feet . . . We should never forget that the way we live and work together is the first and most important way of ministry because this is where the servanthood of Jesus Christ first becomes visible.

Besides the cornerstone which is Christ, the community the Chaplains form with their team is the most important stone in the community they build behind the walls.

Ecumenical working has developed significantly in prison in recent years. The Prison Service Chaplaincy has recently been recognized as a co-ordinating group by Churches Together in England. The Headquarters team has signed an ecumenical covenant, and the church leaders responsible for Chaplaincy work in prison meet regularly together with the three Principal Chaplains and are able to meet and question the Director General and other officials in the service. Ecumenical services are held to dedicate shared chapels. Some appointments to the Chaplaincy are made on a fully ecumenical basis; all Chaplaincy training is ecumenical. A number of prisons have a formal Local Ecumenical Project and all Chaplaincy teams are encouraged to work ecumenically. A member of the Headquarters team acts as Ecumenical Officer and ensures constant attention is paid to that aspect of our working. We have recently recruited and employed a Swedish priest under the Porvoo Agreement.

The Prison Chaplaincy has also acted to facilitate other faiths in prison. Every prisoner is entitled to practise their religion. Most prisons set aside accommodation for the meetings and prayers of non-Christian groups and visiting ministers are appointed for this purpose. For a long time, the Chaplaincy has helped prison staff understand the customs, disciplines and festivals of other faiths. The Prison Service has an obligation to provide for the religious needs of all inmates committed to its care. The arrangements for members of the Buddhist, Hindu, Muslim, Jewish, Sikh, Jain, Bahai's and Chinese religions can be found in *The Directory and Guide on Religious Practices in HM Prisons* and new sections are produced as the need requires. The Prison Service has recently formalized the position of nominating authorities for each of the other faith groups, and has appointed a full-time Muslim Adviser. Although there are still areas of concern, proper channels are in place to ensure an independent determination of need.

Building the church, the faith community behind the walls of prison is a key Chaplaincy task. Most Chaplains run a variety of groups in prison, for discussion and bible study, instruction and personal formation. Alpha Courses are running in 80 of our prisons, and thanks to a generous grant from the Ecclesiastical Insurance Group, a prison co-ordinating team based at Holy Trinity Church, Brompton (HTB) oversees that work. Within the last three years the Kairos/Apac disciplining course has been introduced with significant impact. There is a widespread readership of Christian paperbacks and literature and as part of their 300th celebration SPCK have given each Chaplaincy a significant boost in their theological libraries. YMCA and the Mothers' Union have brought their own skills and talents into the service of those in prison.

The Chaplains' ministry includes Governors and prison staff. All human institutions do things to people. Some prison officers become victims of a system that tends to imprison them and the resulting personal deterioration and tarnished view of human kind are fatal if not infused with new hope. Chaplains need to be actively involved here to encourage, support and share. Equally, they have a right, even a duty, to challenge what appears to them as oppressive, or dehumanizing, always remaining themselves as agents of reconciliation. Many Chaplains take their share of managerial responsibilities in prison. They contribute to offending behaviour, life management programmes, and groups which work with sex offenders and alcohol and drug abuse. The Prison Service is committed to racial equality and, again, many Chaplains take their place on Race Relations Management Teams, ensuring that the Service's policies on race relations are being carried out. In addition Chaplains act as sounding boards for Governors and specialists working in health education and training, helping them, alongside the official reports they prepare, to see individuals against their circumstances and background.

The partnership between the Chaplains and outside faith communities is essential for the success of any Chaplain's ministry. However talented, however powerfully empowered by the Spirit, however strongly mandated by their churches, Chaplains must realize the communal dimension of the new covenant, and their own limitations in representing the outside community. Equally, the Church outside must not lose sight of the sterling ministry and valuable insights which Chaplains discover and display in their daily round.

Most Chaplains work with groups of volunteers who assist with group activities in the Chaplaincy and the regular worship of the chapel. Often these come from particular churches and congregations, encouraged by substitute and part-time Chaplains. Readers can find a good ministry in prison alongside Local Preachers and Probationers. Chaplaincy volunteer organizations develop in this climate of co-operation leading to victim/offender meetings and work with prisoners' families and children. Volunteers staff canteens during visiting hours. Members of the Mothers' Union provide crèche facilities for visiting spouses. Many Chaplains publish a monthly prayer letter. Prison Fellowship sustains 150 local groups and regularly deploys 2,000 volunteers to support and develop Christian ministry to prisoners, ex-prisoners and their families. The independent Prisoners Week group distributed 140,000 leaflets last year, and special services and exhibitions were held in a variety of cathedrals and churches.

Equally significant are the Chaplains' links with the many voluntary groups working in prison. These range from national groups (such as the National Association of Prison Visitors who celebrate their 75th anniversary this year, and provide visitors to any prisoner requiring a visit) to quite small local bands of volunteers, and cover a huge range of concerns: helping prisoners develop personal skills; giving them practical support; assisting in therapeutic work of various kinds and giving help to prisoners' families. Whilst some work within establishments, many work outside to give assistance in rehabilitation and crime prevention, helping prisoners find a better way. As HM Chief Inspector of Prisons put it: 'There are three factors that are said to be most likely to prevent an offender reoffending on release – a job, a home, and a stable relationship.' Volunteers can help in providing all three, and the Prison Chaplain is often an important bridge, as the prisoner moves away from the prison into the world outside.

Chaplains and Boards of Visitors should have a great deal in common, because both share some degree of independence from the system, which is a precious thing and which, if lost, negates something of their special character. Chaplains and Boards, together with perhaps Education Officers, need to be natural allies in this respect, being alongside one another as agents of reform. Again, the need for a real community inside and outside is essential if Chaplains are to be bearers of hope in so many seemingly hopeless and helpless situations.

There are 135 prisons in England and Wales. All have Anglican, Roman Catholic and Methodist Chaplains, together with visiting ministers for other faiths and denominations. Of these, about 140 Church of England Chaplains, 30 Roman Catholic and 6 Methodist Chaplains are full-time. Their numbers include five Church Army Officers, two Readers and a variety of lay and ordained religious (monks and nuns). The Chaplain-General is assisted by four Assistant Chaplains-General, a Principal and a Senior Roman Catholic Chaplain, a seconded Senior Methodist Chaplain covering all Free Church Chaplains and an administrative staff of four.

Chaplains are recruited through open advertisement and attend an assessment centre for selection over a two-day period. The Chaplaincy has set up links between theological colleges and courses and individual prisons, which together with the twice-yearly 'Taster' course it runs at the Prison Service College, gives a useful introduction to prison ministry. Candidates from whatever background are assessed by people who have a working knowledge of the Prison Service, and, if recommended, will be posted to an establishment.

Whilst the Prison Service is a national service, every effort is made to accommodate individual family needs alongside the needs of the service and the particular skills and gifts the individual brings. The Headquarters team give much time and thought to this process.

Wherever possible the first posting is to a deputy post in a large establishment where the new Chaplain can learn the skills of the work alongside others. Sometimes, however, it is necessary to place the individual in a singleton post where support will be given by the local

Chaplaincy team and the appropriate Assistant Chaplain-General. As well as local training, all full-time Chaplains have a mandatory five-year training pattern usually held at the Prison Service College, Newbold Revel. Each Chaplain is also expected to attend an annual retreat, and three or four are arranged each year by the Chaplaincy Training Officer for this purpose. Area meetings of Chaplains provide further support and it is expected that Chaplains will retain strong links with their deaneries and dioceses.

The work of every Chaplain is reviewed annually, usually by the Governor in consultation with the appropriate person in the Chaplaincy Headquarters, and personal objectives are set. In addition, every Chaplaincy team is assessed each year by a formal annual review visit on an ecumenical basis by a member of the Headquarters Team. The reports on those annual review visits are shared with the local church leaders. The Board of Visitors will usually report on the work of their individual Chaplaincy, and the Chaplaincy will be inspected by Her Majesty's Chief Inspector of Prisons when he and his team visit any prison. This complex pattern of selection, training, support, assessment and inspection helps to ensure the high ideals and standards of the Prison Service Chaplaincy.

H. A. Williams in an article on 'Gentleness' wrote:

> Then I am able to accept perversities and failures in other people because I know that I am in the same boat as they are, and that my only hope, like theirs is that God wills to have mercy upon all men. Then I can be of a gentle spirit for I am finding my security not in what I am, but in what God is. Such gentleness towards other people is the way in which Christ sends us into the world, as the Father sent Him. It is the most real and effective form of evangelism . . . when a man feels that somebody accepts him, blemishes and all, without any sort of strings attached, then for that man the Kingdom of God has drawn near with power to heal and raise from the dead.[2]

Coming towards the end of his time as a prisoner, and indeed to the end of his life, Dietrich Bonhoeffer wrote:

> We have been silent witnesses of evil deeds. Many storms have gone over our heads. We have learnt the art of deception and of equivocal speech. Experience has made us suspicious of others, and prevented us from being open and frank. Bitter conflicts have made us weary and even cynical. Are we still serviceable? It is not that genius that we shall need, not the cynic, not the misanthropist, not the adroit tactician, but the honest straightforward men.[3]

The combination of Williams' 'gentleness' and Bonhoeffer's 'straight-forwardness' is essential. Working in the Prison System over the years undoubtedly leaves its mark. Chaplains survive by God's grace, by recognizing the abnormality of what they do, by being a bit uncomfortable about it, by questioning the justification for imprisonment and by seeking to understand why such a system has to exist. They should always remember that the injunction of Jesus, 'When I was in prison you visited me' had no condition attached. And the only person who was ever promised, 'Today you will be with me in paradise', was a convicted thief.

9

A Theology of Vulnerability

Peter Sedgwick

In the preceding pages, we caught a glimpse of what it means to be a vulnerable person in prison today. The reality is much wider than the term 'vulnerable prisoner' or a person on Rule 45, which usually refers to a sex offender or a person at risk from other inmates. This is the definition used by the Prison Service to enable it to segregate someone for his or her own safety. It is understandable that the service will need a fairly tight definition so that they can protect the most vulnerable.

As we know, vulnerability goes far further than this definition. The relationships which make up a person's life are created inside families as a person grows up into an adult. Families who have a member in custody, especially a parent, can suffer damage in profound ways. If that parent in custody is a mother, the damage can be enormous to her children. Young people in custody are especially vulnerable, as the figures for suicide and self-harm show clearly. Young women with children represent a particular challenge. Here, vulnerability can tear a family apart.

Others who are deeply vulnerable are those with mental illness, and those whose sexuality is so warped that they attack or molest others. Sometimes those with mental illness can be fearful and unassertive. Sometimes, they can be strongly aggressive and be a real danger to others as well as to themselves. Paedophiles can conceal their own feelings and manipulate others to convince them that their feelings are the same as other people.

All these individuals are vulnerable. The issue is not whether individuals are attractive or elicit our sympathy, or whether they are a danger to others, but whether they are vulnerable. The degree of danger in the people mentioned above will vary; from the family member who has committed no offence but who has a close relative in custody, through to the person with mental illness who has attacked others. The reason they are all vulnerable is that they are persons whose identity and relationships are deeply affected by their environment. Put simply, where they are affects who they are at the root of their being. In part, that is true of all of us. We are all changed as a result of experiences which can made us more brutalized, less trusting and more insecure. Nick Davies' brilliant study of poverty in England in the 1990s, entitled *Dark Heart* (1997), tells the story of ordinary men and women who descend into a hell of drug addiction, prostitution, crime and unemployment; their personalities and character remain with you long after the book is finished, and the memory of some 'sink estates' stays graphically in the mind. Poverty affects us all deeply and makes us emotionally vulnerable.

Nevertheless, there are some groups of people who are intrinsically more vulnerable as individuals. These chapters spell this out in detail. The opening two chapters by Paul Cavadino and Martin Narey set the idea of vulnerability in context. But it is important that the positive aspects are recognized too. There has been a more constructive approach to the innate problems of offenders in prison in recent years, although this has also been threatened by cutbacks until recently. There is better education planned in the next three years for those who are illiterate; there is co-operation with the Welfare to Work initiative in gaining new job skills; there are strategies for challenging offender behaviour and for bringing people off drugs; there is a rethink of policies on women and young people. This must be set against the harsher climate of public opinion and longer sentencing, well described in detail by Paul Cavadino.

The causes of vulnerability will vary. For young people it is bullying and poor education. Despite the improvements mentioned above, some young people in prison remain very poorly literate. They feel a misfit:

Plate 5: The prison environment brings into sharp focus what it means to be vulnerable. *Jason Shenai, for the Prison Reform Trust.*

they cannot apply for jobs because they cannot read or do simple mathematical tasks. Dyslexia, bullying, a past history of parents not being supportive and stress can create a vulnerable, insecure, often angry and aggressive young person.

For women, once again, there is history of abuse, violence and bullying. Many of them (almost half) had received help for emotional or mental problems in the year before they came into prison. A high proportion take refuge in drugs. The recent television programme *Jailbirds* showed the very sad sight of young teenage girls in prison trying to talk to their mothers on the phone and get some reassurance. The emotional chaos is huge. When there are children, there is even more damage. In spite of this, as the Chaplain at New Hall, Jane Clay, said, there is great warmth and resilience in these prisoners.

Prisoners' families suffer deeply. Children of prisoners are often teased or bullied at school. Visits to prisoners often involve lengthy journeys, and the actual visit can be deeply stressful, especially for children. Sometimes, a prisoner who has failed a drug test will go to meet his family and find that the family have not been told that no physical access is allowed in case of drugs being given to the prisoner. The child turns up and there can be no hug: only a glass wall behind which sits 'Dad'. What does that do to a child?

Prisoners who are mentally ill are further at risk of being stigmatized. The personal view of the psychiatrist writing the chapter on mentally disordered offenders is that every effort should be made to divert them from prison. The appendix on Christopher Edwards is a particularly poignant illustration of the failure to provide alternative accommodation for a person who should never have gone to prison, let alone been killed there.

Those from a minority ethnic background may also be suffering from mental illness, be young, be a woman and have a family inside. Again, *Dark Heart* describes in graphic terms the rejection felt by West Indians arriving as immigrants in Britain in the 1950s, and the painful descent into criminality, pimping and drug dealing of two black families. It ends with the death of one man by drug overdose, and the suicide of another. What is so poignant is the destruction of the high hopes of an immigrant family by racial prejudice and discrimination. Today, there are large numbers of young black people in custody, often with bad experiences of the police. In the light of the Stephen Lawrence Inquiry there is a new mood for change, but it is still early days. The Prison Service has also reaffirmed its strong commitment against racism recently, but it is hard to recruit black and Asian prison officers. Too often white officers guard young black men. It is inherently a difficult situation. There is also the growing question of interfaith relationships between the Christian Chaplain and the visiting Imam or minister from another faith.

Finally, there is the sex offender, who elicits anger and is often despised for the actions which have brought him or her to prison. Tim Newell offers a particularly acute account of the vulnerability of the offender held in segregation. There is also a moving account by an offender in Grendon, John Wrigglesworth, who reflects on his vulnerability, 'no end to grief . . . guilt for the past . . . feel like a kitten . . . my fears . . . isolated'.

This is the world in which the Prison Chaplain ministers. It is a world of raw emotion, blunt feelings and hurt. Into this world of violence and aggression, the prison staff try to prepare prisoners for possible release (depending on their sentence) and for rehabilitation. The Prison Chaplain has his or her own part to play in this. As the chapter on Chaplaincy points out, prisons are places of noise, where life is regimented and the violent rub shoulders with the weak-willed. Only Chaplains who know themselves well emotionally will cope with this work. Only a deep grasp of the Christian faith in one's gut will enable a message of hope to be preached.

The cynic will say that the Chaplain is there to sanctify the restrictions and the segregation which the State places on prisoners. Yet, in informal communication, a Chaplain can hold open the promise of love, hope and a future in which new relationships can be built and old ones mended. Conversations are not a place for indulgence. Informal communication is the key factor, for it is in casual meetings that relationships can be built up. The response to vulnerability is both to affirm the person and to enable them to face up to the past. It is difficult, challenging and intrinsically valuable work. As the article on Chaplaincy says, the chaplain does not work alone. There is a chaplaincy team, there are volunteers who work in prison (sometimes with Chaplains) to help prisoners in many different ways.

In all of this, the reality of vulnerability is the central factor to be addressed. A theology of vulnerability must end with coming face to face with Jesus, vulnerable and dying on the cross, or healing the mentally ill who had taken refuge from society in the graveyard, or affirming the value of the women taken in adultery. Here is a description of a person who encountered vulnerability at every turn and whose response to it led to his being killed. As the nineteenth-century peasant-poet John Clare wrote in rural Cambridgeshire on the ministry of Jesus:

> A stranger once did bless the earth
>   who never caused a heart to mourn,
> Whose very voice gave sorrow mirth;
>   and how did earth his worth return?
> It spurned him from its lowliest lot:
> The meanest station owned him not.

We should remember that Clare, one of the finest nineteenth-century nature poets and a devout Christian, ended up confined in a lunatic asylum, where his pathetic insights into his pitiful condition were not enough to enable him to regain sanity and freedom. He died in the asylum. Modern society can treat psychiatric illness in far better ways than confinement, but there are still many in prison today, aching for their family, confused, vulnerable and held behind bars.

There are some valuable reflections on this theme in *Wales: A Moral Society?*, the report produced by a group chaired by Bishop Rowan Williams and published by CYTÛN (Churches Together in Wales) in June 1996. God's action in the biblical story is characterized by self-giving. God works not by dominance and power but by becoming vulnerable to others in love. God is not self-protective, but generous. We lose God's image if we are locked into defensiveness, selfishness and a struggle for survival. God communicates by fragile human acts and words.

> If God's image is to be realised in us, we must be capable . . . of taking risks . . . We have to come to terms with our own vulnerability, the vulnerability that we discover in being committed to each other. If people are constantly being pressed to insure against their vulnerability, to withdraw from commitment so as to preserve their own safety, God becomes less visible.[1]

This suggests that being vulnerable is in fact to be like God. This is a hard thing to say in prison, where to be vulnerable means having a weakness (youth, mental illness, family tie) which the Prison System can tear apart. That sort of vulnerability is to be guarded against at all costs: we need fewer suicides, fewer depressed young women, fewer confused people with mental illness in prison. Nevertheless, the Christian message is that the grace of God is most fully seen in weakness (2 Corinthians 12.8).

There are, it may be suggested, two sorts of vulnerability, as there are, by analogy, two sorts of poverty. There is enforced poverty, made up of low income, resources, damp housing and few prospects for change. Such poverty, as Nick Davies points out, causes emotional damage, and makes people vulnerable. He writes in *Dark Heart,* 'The teachers sometimes ask the children what they want to be when they grow up, and inevitably they hear the same answer: "Nothing".'

There is another sort of poverty, which is that voluntarily embraced by the young rich man Francis of Assisi. He called it 'Sister Poverty' and it meant the renunciation of the way in which wealth, fashion and status could become ends in themselves, and so be all-encompassing. The person becomes selfish, concerned with their appearance at the expense of inner integrity and personal growth. He decided that it would be better to seek a life of true simplicity, finding in his freely chosen poverty the way to come close to nature, to other people and to the God whose Son 'had nowhere to lay his head'. The example of St Francis has inspired people for centuries in his poverty and inner joy. Poverty is an analogy to vulnerability. The freely chosen vulnerability and poverty of Francis is found in the humanity of contemporary saints, who have died to be near the people they love or have given away their possessions. This is different from enforced vulnerability. Enforced vulnerability is not lifegiving; it goes with being impressionable, as many who work with deprived and vulnerable young people know. The harsh world of the prison can easily take such people and mould them into individuals with a long criminal career ahead of them, despite the best efforts of prison staff.

That is why the essays in this book have given two simple messages. One is that the vulnerable should not be in prison at all, but serve community sentences. To adapt a phrase, 'prison is an expensive way of making vulnerable people worse'. That is the clear message of Paul Cavadino's article and many others. The second message is that conditions urgently need to be improved. The Prison Service has made a start, but there is much to do and at times in the 1990s things appeared to be going backwards, with cuts in education, skills training and in recreation.

There is no doubt that enforced vulnerability destroys people. It is vulnerability enforced by upbringing, circumstances and fragile relationships. Put such a person in a prison and the result is depression, violence, even death by suicide or the attacks of others. The paradox is that the Christian message, while always seeking to end enforced vulnerability, speaks of embracing a freely chosen vulnerability. Such a theology has been articulated by several recent Anglican theologians, including Peter Baelz and William Vanstone. It is, in essence, a theology of the vulnerability of God.

Vanstone refers to the ceaseless activity of the modern world and its commitment to 'the flag of independence and individual enterprise and personal achievement and unceasing activism: and under these colours we sail courageously but perhaps ill-advisedly into a future in which, to an ever-increasing degree, the system will dominate the individual'.[2] What is needed is to rediscover the unique dignity of being open, vulnerable and passive to the glory of the world. Vanstone speaks of the vulnerability of being affected by the environment and says that the suffering of Jesus – his passion – comes from the Greek for being affected: πασχω (pasco) or 'to be done to'. The passion of Jesus is not strictly speaking his suffering, but that He was exposed to others. In this being handed over to the mercy of others, the vulnerability of Jesus is laid bare.[3]

So what implication do we draw from this freely chosen vulnerability? Peter Baelz in *Does God Answer Prayer?* (1982) speaks of the analogy of love in the way God works with his world. He is vulnerable, open and loving, seeking a response which is free and responsible from others. Prayer will not cause the world to 'behave as if it were subject to a powerful and external manipulation . . . Prayer is not a special spiritual force.' What God's love can do is to venture 'All it can by arousing interest, awakening desires and winning a response'. Such a commitment makes God very vulnerable. As Peter Baelz says, God achieves his purposes by first sending Jesus, and then us in the name of Jesus Christ. 'It all depends on us, and we depend on God.'

There are, then, in conclusion, two sorts of vulnerability. There is enforced vulnerability, which hurts, breaks and is at risk in the world of the prison. This collection of essays is designed to show what the cost of imprisonment actually is. Then, secondly, there is the Christian hope and the freely chosen vulnerability of love. This is neither sentimental nor cowardly. It requires great strength to live out that vulnerability, and prison is a place where people shut down their responses to others in order that they may simply survive. What lies behind many of the chapters here, are a series of unspoken strategies. People cope and survive by not showing their feelings, and they put on an act. It is difficult to express a freely chosen vulnerability when you are at risk, anyway, as a young person or a person with mental illness. Prisons create a tough environment with much humour and engagement with others in a boisterous way, but they are not places where deep inner feelings are easily shown. We should be grateful for the ministry of Chaplains, volunteers and staff that enable the vulnerability of love to be shown in such a harsh world.

Notes

Introduction

1.   William Noblett, *Prayers for People in Prison*, OUP, 1998.

Chapter 2: Improvements in Prison Regimes

1.   Jack Straw, *Making Prisons Work*, The Prison Reform Trust Annual Lecture, 1998.

2.   William Temple, *The Ethics of Penal Action*, The First Clarke Hall Lecture, London, 1934.

Chapter 3: Children in Prison

1.   Both the UN Convention on the Rights of the Child and the Children Act 1989 define a child as being under the age of 18.

2.   Prison Service statistics, 1997.

3.   Ibid.

4.   Ibid.

5.   *Misspent Youth*, Audit Commission, 1997.

6.   See *The Howard League Troubleshooter Project: Lessons for Policy and Practice on 15-year-olds in Prison*, 1997; *Lost Inside:The Imprisonment of Teenage Girls*, 1997; and *Sentenced to Fail*, 1998. Published by the Howard League.

7.   *Misspent Youth*, Audit Commission, 1997.

8.   *Young Prisoners:A Thematic Review*, HM Inspector of Prisons for England and Wales, October 1997.

9.   Ibid., para. 5.28.

10.   *Troubleshooter Report*, Howard League, 1997.

11.   *Sentenced to Fail*, Howard League, 1997.

12. *Young Prisoners: A Thematic Review*, op. cit.

13. *Troubleshooter Project*, Howard League, 1997.

14. *Lost Inside: The Imprisonment of Teenage Girls*, Howard League, 1997.

15. *Troubleshooter Project*, op.cit.

16. *Young Prisoners: A Thematic Review*, op. cit.

17. *Young Prisoners: A Thematic Review*, op. cit., para. 4.50, p. 37.

18. *Misspent Youth*, op. cit.

19. Censored against the author's wishes.

20. Prison Service Suicide Awareness Unit.

21. *Young Prisoners: A Thematic Review*, op. cit.

22. Criminal Justice and Public Order Act, 1994.

Chapter 4: Women in Prison

1. A. Morris *et al.*, *Managing the Needs of Female Prisoners*, Home Office, 1995.

2. N. Singleton, H. Meltzer and R. Gatward, *Psychiatric Morbidity Among Prisoners in England and Wales*, Office for National Statistics, 1997.

3. *Women in Prison: A Thematic Review*, HM Inspector of Prisons for England and Wales, 1997.

4. *Women Prisoners*, Penal Affairs Consortium, 1998.

5. HM Prison Service, Strategic Planning Unit fax to Prison Reform Trust, 12 March 1999.

6. Prison Statistics in England and Wales, 1997.

7. Ibid.

8. Ibid.

9. Ibid.

10. N. Singleton *et al.*, op. cit.

11. HM Prison Service, Health Care Standards for Prisons in England and Wales.

12. HM Prison Service, Drug Misuse in Prison.

13. HM Prison Service, Health Care Standards for Prisons in England and Wales.

14. HM Prison Service, Submission to Woolf Inquiry into Prison Disturbances, 1990.

15. Quoted in A. Devlin, *Invisible Women*, Waterside Press, 1998.

16. HM Inspectorate of Prisons, 1998.

17. *Women Prisoners: A safer Way*, Social Work Services and Prisons Inspectorate for Scotland, 1998.

Chapter 5: Mentally Disordered Offenders

1. A. Maden, C. Taylor, D. Brooke and J. Gunn, *Mental Disorder in Remand Prisoners*, a Report commissioned by the Home Office Research and Planning Unit on behalf of The Directorate of Health Care, 1996.

2. J. Gunn, A. Maden and M. Swinton, *Mentally Disordered Prisoners*, Department of Forensic Psychiatry, Institute of Psychiatry, London, 1991.

3. L. Teplin, 'The prevalence of severe mental disorder among male urban jail detainees: comparison with the epidemiologic catchment area programme', *American Journal of Public Health*, 80 (1990), 663–9.

4. N. Singleton, H. Meltzer and R. Gatward, *Psychiatric Morbidity among Prisoners in England and Wales*, Office for National Statistics, 1997.

5. A. Maden *et al.*, op. cit.

6. A. Maden *et al.*, op. cit.

7. J. Gunn and P. J. Taylor, *Forensic Psychiatry: Clinical, Legal and Ethical Issues*, London, Butterworth Heinemann, 1993.

8. T. Bennett, *Drug Testing Arrestees*, Home Office Research and Statistics Directorate, Research Findings no. 70, 1998.

9. E. Edgar and I. O'Donnell, *Mandatory Drug Testing in Prisons: An Evaluation*, Home Office Research and Statistics Directorate, Research Findings no. 75, 1996.

10. I. O'Donnell and K. Edgar, *Victimisation in Prisons*, Home Office Research and Statistics Directorate, Research Findings no. 37, 1996.

Chapter 7: Prisoners' Families

1. J. Ditchfield, *Family Ties and Recidivism: Main Findings of the Literature*, Home Office Research Bulletin no. 36, 1994.

2. R. Burnett, *The Dynamics of Recidivism*, Oxford Centre for Criminological Research, unpublished report to the Home Office, 1992.

3. *My Dad's in Prison* and *My Mum's in Prison*, series of information leaflets.

Chapter 8: Prison Chaplaincy

1. Alan Paton, *Too Late the Phalarope*, Scribners, 1953, pp. 264–5.

2. H.A. Williams, 'Gentleness', *Theology*, September 1962.

3. Dietrich Bonhoeffer, *Letters and Papers from Prison*, SCM Press, 1953, Fontana edition, p. 148.

Chapter 9: A Theology of Vulnerability

1. *Wales: A Moral Society?*, Churches Together in Wales, 1996, p.5.

2. William Vanstone, *The Stature of Waiting*, Darton, Longman & Todd, 1982, p. 110.

3. Ibid., pp. 30–33.

Further Reading

Journals

HLM, Howard League for Penal Reform, quarterly.

Prison Report, Prison Reform Trust, quarterly.

Prison Fellowship News, Prison Fellowship, quarterly.

Safer Society, NACRO, quarterly.

Reports

Board for Social Responsibility, *Private Sector Involvement in Prisons*, Church House Publishing, 1996.

Catholic Agency for Social Concern, *Women in Prison*, 1999.

Oxford Diocesan Board for Social Responsibility, *Beyond Redemption?*, Oxford, 1997.

Oxford Diocesan Board for Social Responsibility, *Minority Ethnic Issues for Criminal Justice*, Oxford, 1999.

Publications

J. Burnside and N. Baker (eds.), *Relational Justice*, Waterside Press, 1994.

George Carey, 'Restoring Relationships: The Purpose of Prisons', Prison Reform Trust Annual Lecture, 1996.

T. Gorringe, *God's Just Vengeance: A Theology of Imprisonment*, Cambridge University Press, 1996.

William Noblett, *Prayers for People in Prison*, OUP, 1998.

Vivien Stern, *A Sin Against the Future: Imprisonment in the World*, Penguin, 1998.

Chris Wood (ed.), *The End of Punishment: Christian Perspectives on the Crisis in Criminal Justice*, St Andrew Press, Edinburgh, 1991.

Contacts

Bourne Trust (Roman Catholic – supports prisoners' families)
1–3 Brixton Road, London SW9 6DE; Tel: 020 7582 6659.

Howard League for Penal Reform
708 Holloway Road, London N19 3NL; Tel: 020 7288 7722.

Langley House Trust (for ex-offenders – Christian based)
46 Market Square, Witney, Oxon OX8 6AL; Tel: 01993 774 075.

NACRO (National Association for the Care and Resettlement of Offenders)
169 Clapham Road, London SW9 0PU; Tel: 020 7582 6500.

Prison Fellowship (Christian ministry)
PO Box 945, Maldon, Essex CM9 4EW; Tel: 01621 843 232.

Prison Reform Trust
15 Northburgh Street, London EC1V 0AH; Tel: 020 7251 5070.

Mothers' Union (Anglican – supports prisoners' families)
Mary Sumner House, 24 Tufton Street, London SW1P 3RB;
Tel: 020 7222 5533.

Social Concern (Anglican – campaigns for alternatives to prison
and Restorative Justice)
Montague Chambers, Montague Close, London SE1 9DA;
Tel: 020 7403 0977.

Catholic Agency for Social Concern (CASC)
39 Eccleston Square, London SW1V 1BX; Tel: 020 7828 4371.

Federation of Prisoners' Families Support Group
Cambridge House, Cambridge Grove, London W9; Tel: 020 8741 4578.